Communications
in Computer and Information Science 1908

Rationale

The CCIS series is devoted to the publication of proceedings of computer science conferences. Its aim is to efficiently disseminate original research results in informatics in printed and electronic form. While the focus is on publication of peer-reviewed full papers presenting mature work, inclusion of reviewed short papers reporting on work in progress is welcome, too. Besides globally relevant meetings with internationally representative program committees guaranteeing a strict peer-reviewing and paper selection process, conferences run by societies or of high regional or national relevance are also considered for publication.

Topics

The topical scope of CCIS spans the entire spectrum of informatics ranging from foundational topics in the theory of computing to information and communications science and technology and a broad variety of interdisciplinary application fields.

Information for Volume Editors and Authors

Publication in CCIS is free of charge. No royalties are paid, however, we offer registered conference participants temporary free access to the online version of the conference proceedings on SpringerLink (http://link.springer.com) by means of an http referrer from the conference website and/or a number of complimentary printed copies, as specified in the official acceptance email of the event.

CCIS proceedings can be published in time for distribution at conferences or as post-proceedings, and delivered in the form of printed books and/or electronically as USBs and/or e-content licenses for accessing proceedings at SpringerLink. Furthermore, CCIS proceedings are included in the CCIS electronic book series hosted in the SpringerLink digital library at http://link.springer.com/bookseries/7899. Conferences publishing in CCIS are allowed to use Online Conference Service (OCS) for managing the whole proceedings lifecycle (from submission and reviewing to preparing for publication) free of charge.

Publication process

The language of publication is exclusively English. Authors publishing in CCIS have to sign the Springer CCIS copyright transfer form, however, they are free to use their material published in CCIS for substantially changed, more elaborate subsequent publications elsewhere. For the preparation of the camera-ready papers/files, authors have to strictly adhere to the Springer CCIS Authors' Instructions and are strongly encouraged to use the CCIS LaTeX style files or templates.

Abstracting/Indexing

CCIS is abstracted/indexed in DBLP, Google Scholar, EI-Compendex, Mathematical Reviews, SCImago, Scopus. CCIS volumes are also submitted for the inclusion in ISI Proceedings.

How to start

To start the evaluation of your proposal for inclusion in the CCIS series, please send an e-mail to ccis@springer.com.

Cédric Grueau · Robert Laurini · Lemonia Ragia
Editors

Geographical Information Systems Theory, Applications and Management

7th International Conference, GISTAM 2021
Virtual Event, April 23–25, 2021
and 8th International Conference, GISTAM 2022
Virtual Event, April 27–29, 2022
Revised Selected Papers

 Springer

Editors
Cédric Grueau
Polytechnic Institute of Setúbal/IPS
Setúbal, Portugal

Robert Laurini
Knowledge Systems Institute
Skokie, IL, USA

Lemonia Ragia
ATHENA Research & Innovation
Information Technologies
Marousi, Greece

ISSN 1865-0929   ISSN 1865-0937 (electronic)
Communications in Computer and Information Science
ISBN 978-3-031-44111-0   ISBN 978-3-031-44112-7 (eBook)
https://doi.org/10.1007/978-3-031-44112-7

This Springer imprint is published by the registered company Springer Nature Switzerland AG
The registered company address is: Gewerbestrasse 11, 6330 Cham, Switzerland

Paper in this product is recyclable.

Preface

The present book includes extended and revised versions of a set of selected papers from the 7th and 8th International Conferences on Geographical Information Systems Theory, Applications and Management (GISTAM 2021 and GISTAM 2022), exceptionally held as web-based events, due to the COVID-19 pandemic, from 23–25 April 2021 and 27–29 April 2022, respectively.

GISTAM 2021 received 44 paper submissions from 24 countries, of which 9% were included in this book. GISTAM 2022 received 27 paper submissions from 20 countries, of which 11% were included in this book.

The papers were selected by the event chairs and their selection was based on a number of criteria that include classifications and comments provided by program committee members, session chairs' assessment and also the program chairs' global view of all the papers included in the technical program. The authors of selected papers were then invited to submit revised and extended versions of their papers having at least 30% innovative material.

The International Conference on Geographical Information Systems Theory, Applications and Management aims to create a meeting point of researchers and practitioners that address new challenges in geo-spatial data sensing, observation, representation, processing, visualization, sharing and managing, in all aspects concerning both information communication and technologies (ICT) as well as management information systems and knowledge-based systems. The conference welcomes original papers of either practical or theoretical nature, presenting research or applications, of specialized or interdisciplinary nature, addressing any aspect of geographic information systems and technologies.

The papers selected to be included in this book contribute to the understanding of relevant trends of current research on Geographical Information Systems Theory, Applications and Management, including: Disaster Management and Deep Learning for Urban and Environment Planning, Earth Observation and Satellite Data and Decision Support Systems, Ecological and Environmental Management, Energy Information Systems, Geospatial Information and Technologies, GPS and Location Detection, Machine Learning for Spatial Data, Natural Resource Management, Performance Evaluation, RADAR and LiDAR, Remote Sensing of Agriculture, Spatial Analysis and Integration, Spatial Information and Society, Spectroscopy and Spectroradiometry, Topological Modeling and Analysis, Urban and Regional Planning, and Urban Remote Sensing.

We would like to thank all the authors for their contributions and also the reviewers who have helped to ensure the quality of this publication.

April 2022

Cédric Grueau
Robert Laurini
Lemonia Ragia

Organization

Conference Chair

Lemonia Ragia — ATHENA Research & Innovation Center in Information Technologies, Greece

Program Co-chairs

2021

Cédric Grueau — Polytechnic Institute of Setúbal/IPS, Portugal
Robert Laurini (Honorary) — Knowledge Systems Institute, France

2022

Cédric Grueau — Polytechnic Institute of Setúbal/IPS, Portugal

Program Committee

2021

Andrea Ajmar	Politecnico di Torino, Italy
Rute Almeida	University of Porto, Portugal
José António-Tenedório	Universidade NOVA de Lisboa, Portugal
Thierry Badard	Laval University, Canada
Jan Blachowski	Wroclaw University of Science and Technology, Poland
Pedro Cabral	Nanjing University of Information Science and Technology, China
Cristina Catita	Universidade de Lisboa, Portugal
Filiberto Chiabrando	Politecnico di Torino, Italy
Eliseo Clementini	University of L'Aquila, Italy
Antonio Corral	University of Almería, Spain
Paolo Dabove	Politecnico di Torino, Italy
Pinliang Dong	University of North Texas, USA

Massimiliano Pepe	Politecnico di Bari, Italy
Muhammad Zulkarnain bin Rahman	Universiti Teknologi Malaysia, Malaysia
Dar A. Roberts	University of California, Santa Barbara, USA
Mathieu Roche	Cirad, France
John Samuel	Graduate School of Chemistry, Physics and Electronics, Lyon, France
Diego Seco	Universidade da Coruña, Spain
Sylvie Servigne	INSA Lyon, France
Yosio Shimabukuro	Instituto Nacional de Pesquisas Espaciais, Brazil
Francesco Soldovieri	Consiglio Nazionale delle Ricerche, Italy
Uwe Stilla	Technische Universität München, Germany
Jantien Stoter	Delft University of Technology, The Netherlands
Rui Sun	Beijing Normal University, China
Ana Teodoro	Oporto University, Portugal
Fabio Tosti	University of West London, UK
Goce Trajcevski	Northwestern University, USA
Michael Vassilakopoulos	University of Thessaly, Volos, Greece
Benoit Vozel	University of Rennes I - IETR/Shine, France
Lei Wang	Louisiana State University, USA
Christiane Weber	UMR TETIS CNRS, Maison de la Télédétection, France
Stephan Winter	University of Melbourne, Australia
Laszlo Zentai	Eötvos-Lorand University, Hungary
F. Benjamin Zhan	Texas State University, USA

2022

Andrea Ajmar	Politecnico di Torino, Italy
Thierry Badard	Laval University, Canada
Pete Bettinger	University of Georgia, USA
Jan Blachowski	Wroclaw University of Science and Technology, Poland
Pedro Cabral	Nanjing University of Information Science and Technology, China
Cristina Catita	Universidade de Lisboa, Portugal
Filiberto Chiabrando	Politecnico di Torino, Italy
Eliseo Clementini	University of L'Aquila, Italy
Antonio Corral	University of Almería, Spain
Paolo Dabove	Politecnico di Torino, Italy
Vincenzo Di Pietra	Politecnico di Torino, Italy
Anastasios Doulamis	National Technical University of Athens, Greece

Nikolaos Doulamis	National Technical University of Athens, Greece
João Fernandes	Universidade de Lisboa, Portugal
Cheng Fu	University of Zurich, Switzerland
Sébastien Gadal	Aix-Marseille University, CNRS ESPACE UMR 7300, France and North-Eastern Federal University, Russia
Nicholas K. G. Garrett	Auckland University of Technology, New Zealand
Ioannis Gitas	Aristotle University of Thessaloniki, Greece
Fabio Giulio Tonolo	Politecnico di Torino, Italy
Hans Guesgen	Massey University, New Zealand
Cristina Henriques	University of Lisbon, Portugal
Stephen Hirtle	University of Pittsburgh, USA
Wen-Chen Hu	University of North Dakota, USA
Karsten Jacobsen	Leibniz Universität Hannover, Germany
Simon Jirka	52°North GmbH, Germany
Roberto Lattuada	myHealthbox, Italy
Vladimir Lukin	Kharkov Aviation Institute, Ukraine
Jean Mas	Universidad Nacional Autónoma de México, Mexico
Gavin McArdle	University College Dublin, Ireland
Gintautas Mozgeris	Vytautas Magnus University, Lithuania
Anand Nayyar	Duy Tan University, Vietnam
Dimos Pantazis	University of West Attica, Greece
Cesar Parcero-Oubiña	Spanish National Research Council (CSIC), Spain
Dar A. Roberts	University of California, Santa Barbara, USA
Mathieu Roche	Cirad, France
Shouraseni Sen Roy	University of Miami, USA
John Samuel	Graduate School of Chemistry, Physics and Electronics, Lyon, France
Diego Seco	Universidade da Coruña, Spain
Elif Sertel	Istanbul Technical University, Turkey
Sylvie Servigne	INSA Lyon, France
Yosio Shimabukuro	Instituto Nacional de Pesquisas Espaciais, Brazil
Ana Teodoro	Oporto University, Portugal
Lorenzo Teppati Losè	Politecnico di Torino, Italy
Fabio Tosti	University of West London, UK
Goce Trajcevski	Northwestern University, USA
Benoit Vozel	University of Rennes I - IETR/Shine, France
Lei Wang	Louisiana State University, USA
Christiane Weber	UMR TETIS CNRS, Maison de la Télédétection, France
Tahsin Yomralioglu	Istanbul Technical University, Turkey

Le Yu · Tsinghua University, China
Laszlo Zentai Eötvos-Lorand University, Hungary

Additional Reviewers

2021

Ana Navarro University of Lisbon, Portugal
Hamidreza Rabiei-Dastjerdi University College Dublin, Ireland

Invited Speakers

2021

Ioannis Manakos Centre for Research and Technology Hellas,
Greece
Toshihiro Osaragi Tokyo Institute of Technology, Japan
Lena Halounova Czech Technical University in Prague, Czech
Republic

2022

Niki Evelpidou National and Kapodistrian University of Athens,
Greece
Ahmet C. Yalciner Middle East Technical University, Turkey
Dimitri Konstantas University of Geneva, Switzerland

Contents

Mapping Prosopis Juliflora Invasion Using Remote Sensing Data and GIS Geostatistics Techniques

Alya Almaazmi[✉], Rami Al-Ruzouq, and Abdallah Shanableh

University of Sharjah, Sharjah, UAE
U20104130@sharjah.ac.ae

Abstract. Prosopis Juliflora is a highly invasive tree that has a severe impact on native species and ecosystems. The most difficult part of controlling Prosopis Juliflora invasion is precisely mapping its presence and distribution pattern. Recent developments in remote sensing and geographic information system (GIS) technologies have enabled to map different types of vegetation. In this study, remote sensing data were combined with supervised classification using a Support Vector Machine (SVM) to map the total cover of Prosopis Juliflora, which was then analyzed using a GIS geo-statistical system. In Sharjah, the UAE's third largest city, images from Landsat 7 and 8 were used over the years 2000, 2010, and 2020. The overall cover of Prosopis Juliflora increased by 1.17% during 20 years, from 11.99 km^2 in 2000 to 14.13 km^2 in 2020, according to Prosopis Juliflora maps. Geo-statistics showed that Prosopis Juliflora exhibits a spatial clustering pattern and that the majority of Prosopis Juliflora is still under controllable secondary scheme in the eastern and southern parts of the city, with the exception of some areas in the eastern and western parts of the city that require thinning.

Keywords: Remote sensing · GIS · Prosopis Juliflora · Vegetation · Statistics

1 Introduction

Invasive species (also known as alien, exotic, or non-native species) are any taxa species that colonize biogeographic barriers of their natural range with or without human interface [1, 2].They are also characterized as species that have adverse impacts on native biodiversity, such as alternating an entire ecosystem processes [3]. Because of their economic, environmental, or aesthetic benefits, alien plant species have been introduced all over the world. However, introducing new species is not always likely to succeed. One of the complications associated is the risk of the species becoming invasive. For example, It is believed that 1% to 2% of exotic become invasive weeds [4]. Invasive impacts are often classified as environmental, economic, or social costs. Environmental impacts are related to ecosystem structure and function, and are frequently associated with biodiversity loss or the loss of distinctive native habitats. Moreover, human health, safety, and quality of life are the primary concerns of social repercussions. On the other hand, economically,

C. Grueau et al. (Eds.): GISTAM 2021/2022, CCIS 1908, pp. 1–15, 2023.
https://doi.org/10.1007/978-3-031-44112-7_1

the impacts are directly related to monetary losses [5]. Due to their irrevocable impact, invasive species became a contemporary focus of concern for ecologists, biological conservationists, and natural managers [6]. Several international organizations have made the issue of invasive plants a priority in their work and developed management and education recommendations [7–9].

Prosopis Juliflora is without a doubt one of the most persistent and resistant invasive plant species that are growing at an alarming rate in the arid and sub-arid regions of the planet. The Tree is originally native to Central America, the Caribbean, and Northern South America [10]. The tree can thrive in arid climates and marginal soils conditions where few other plants could survive. Every portion of the tree might be used for a variety of things, including fuel, food, medicine, and cosmetics [11, 12]. It was later introduced into North-East Brazil, Bolivia, Colombia, El Salvador, Nicaragua, Uruguay, Venezuela, the West Indies, and the Bahamas as a result of its popularity. It can now be found throughout Asia, Africa, and arid and semi-arid regions of the Americas [13].

Prosopis Juliflora is a deciduous leguminous tree that can reach a height of 10–15 m. With an open canopy, the crown is considered large. The leaves are light green, deciduous, geminate-pinnate, and have 12 to 20 leaflets. Florets are 5–10 cm long cylindrical spikes that appear in clusters of 2–5 at the terminals of branches and are characterized as greenish-white turning pale yellow [14]. The pods are 20 to 30 cm long and contain 10 to 30 seeds each pod. A mature plant can yield hundreds of thousands of seeds. Seeds have a ten-year shelf life. Only seeds, not vegetative reproduction, are used to propagate the tree. Seeds are distributed by cattle and other animals by chewing seed pods and distributing seeds in their droppings [15]. Prosopis Juliflora also known as Mesquite have a deep taproot and woody growth beneath the ground It has been shown to be capable of extracting water from the water table down to a depth of 35 m [16].

Prosopis Juliflora is commonly introduced for the intention of forestation, landscape greening, and desertification control, however, there are several potential disadvantages towards introducing Prosopis Juliflora. Environmentally, Prosopis Juliflora unleached and leached Acacia or (litter) in soil, is known to have Allelopathy impact to inhabit other plant species' seeds from germinating in its vicinity [17]. The studies showed that the leaf may contain water-soluble allelochemicals that are drained to the ground as water table drops [18]. Prosopis Juliflora also exhibits autotoxicity, as its leachates prevent its own seeds from germinating. This is presumably one of Prosopis Juliflora survival strategy for preventing its sister trees from growing too close to it and threatening each other's nutrient and water availability [19, 20]. Furthermore, Prosopis Juliflora is responsible for significant biodiversity loss. As the invasion of Prosopis Juliflora progresses, the diversity of native woody species varies inversely [21]. For example, grazing and other forms of anthropogenic disturbances, had a major detrimental impact on the ridge's vegetation diversity in a research on the plant community composition on Delhi ridge [22]. One of the serious environmental issues associated with Prosopis Juliflora is related to water resources. The aggressively growing downward tap roots expansion on water bodies obstructs drainage and aggravate flooding, resulting a deep splits in the ground [23]. Prosopis Juliflora showed unfavorable social influence, particularly in terms of human health. Pollens from Prosopis Juliflora, for example, have been linked to allergic asthma, rhinitis, and skin allergies [24], complicated with climate conditions such as high temperature and dry seasons [25]. Furthermore, the thorns of the Prosopis tree have been implicated in a number of studies as a cause of flesh-related injuries that have resulted in human deaths. Prosopis thorns are exceptionally strong and lengthy, and when punctured, they pierce the skin and enter deep into the flesh. Deep pricks from Prosopis thorns are said to induce itching, and wounds can lead to lameness and amputation due to significant infection [26]. Economically, The most frequently reported detrimental consequences include the loss of agricultural land and the resulting loss of crops that were previously planted in the area, as well as the loss of grazing land and livestock production, in addition to restrictions on human mobility and transportation [27, 28]. Studies also showed another economical dementias in terms of householding. Clearing the fields covered by Prosopis Juliflora and converting some of the invaded grazing lands into agricultural land has resulted in better harvest for households in the invaded area [29].

Major efforts have been indeed put into establishing strategies for studying Prosopis Juliflora ecological and social indicators through direct field sampling and questionnaire-based surveys [30], to evaluate the impact of Prosopis Juliflora and its extension. Although surveys would provide the most complete information, however, invasive species surveys tend to require more person hours to complete, over longer duration time [31]. Furthermore, manual quantifying does not reflect real cases as it considers ecological and social characteristics as a sole unit, without considering the interaction and relationship with the environmental behavior or the spatial and temporal information.

Prosopis Juliflora's aggressive behavior has inspired researchers to establish a scientific effort based on remote sensing data and the Geographic Information System (GIS). Data from remote sensing can cover larger areas than single plot investigations. [32], furthermore, remote sensing provides a valuable opportunity for timely information on non-native species invasions into native environments.. Previous efforts s in mapping Prosopis Juliflora using remote sensing data using spectral indices and classification is acknowledged and summarized in table 6.

The key problem with invasive species is identifying new potential risk places that may be affected similarly [33]. For this purposes, spatial autocorrelation reflects an invasion concern if it is relatively high at certain locations [34]. The spatial dependency of invasive and non-invasive distributions, for example, might be examined using Moran's I spatial autocorrelation test. [35], In addition to Moran's I eigenvector mapping, generalized additive models, and Bayesian intrinsic conditional autoregressive models, there are Bayesian intrinsic conditional autoregressive models. These strategies have been successful in analyzing invasions such as the red swamp crayfish invasion [36]. Moran I, as a measure of spatial autocorrelation at scales of 2–30 m and plotted against lag distance in each transect, might also be used to estimate the spatial scale of habitat clustering of invasive plant species of highways [37] (Table 1).

Although spatial autocorrelation based on feature locations, for each individual feature, only the neighboring values are included in the analysis. Alternatively, The Gi* hot spot analysis provides assessment on local areas with high concentration of a phenomenon within the landscape statistically significant spatial clusters [47]. The value of each feature is included in its own analysis where the local mean for Getis-Ord Gi*

Table 1. Detection and mapping P. Juliflora from remote sensing data.

Study Area	Year	Remote Sensing Data	Methodology	Reference
Pakistan	2021	EO-I Hyperion	Derivative Vegetation Index and Spectral Angle Mapper	[38]
Kenya	2019	Landsat TM 5 Landsat 8	random forest supervised classification	[39]
India	2017	IRS-P6	NDVI and support vector machine supervised classification	[40]
Somaliland	2017	Landsat 8	NDVI and random forest supervised classification	[41]
Somaliland	2015	Landsat 8 Worldview 2	NDVI and maximum likelihood supervised classification	[42]
India	2015	Landsat ETM + 7	NDII	[43]
UAE	2015	Aerial photograph	Manual digitizing	[44]
Ethiopia	2014	MODIS	NDVI and maximum entropy supervised classification	[45]
Sudan	2011	Landsat TM 5 ALOS/PALSAR	NDII and backscattering model	[46]

includes all features. Hot spot has been used widely indeed in analyzing species invasion. In Austria, invasion hotspots where studied under current and future climate [48]. Similarly, in the United States, hotspot analysis along with records of occurrence used to evaluate 70 terrestrial invasive plants [49].

2   Study Area

The study focused on Sharjah city, the third largest emirate in the UAE with an area of 2590 km2. The city is located at 25.3463° N, 55.4209° E, and shares boarder with major cities in UAE such as Ajman and Dubai from the north and south, in addition, it is boarded with Arabian Gulf from the west. The UAE is situated in an arid tropical region, the climate of the region is characterized as hot and dry [50], with an average annual precipitation of 80–140 mm [51]. The wet season occurs between November and March, and an intense dry season extends between the months of June and August. Sharjah averages about 107 mm of rain each year. Deserts, thick soil produced by eolian sands, and some agricultural areas, as well as marshes and acacia woods, cover much of the emirate. The Batinah Coast, which stretches between the mountains and the sea in the southern portion of Sharjah, is a continuous, well-watered fertile coastal strip (Fig. 1).

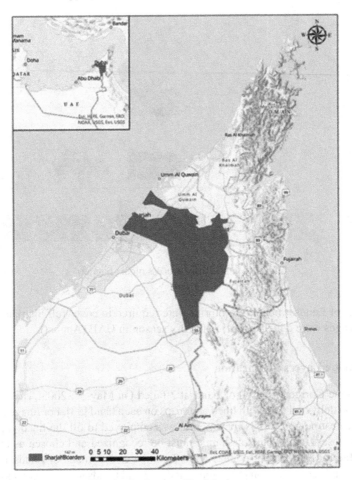

Fig. 1. Study area: Sharjah city map.

3   Methodology

The methodological framework employed in this study to construct the approach in the study area Sharjah city – UAE [52], is illustrated in Fig. 2. First, the data were collected from Landsat 7 and Landsat 8 satellite images. The data were used to construct thematic layers represented as surface reflectance of each multispectral band. There are two primary phases to the methods used: Prosopis Juliflora mapping, and geostatistics and modelling. In the first phase, mapping Prosopis Juliflora is carries through supervised classification. The second phase, Prosopis Juliflora maps were used to perform geostatistical modelling.

3.1   Data Source

Multi-spectral Landsat satellite images were used. The data were collected from Landsat 7 over year 2000 and 2010, while and Landsat 8 used to acquire data over year 2020.

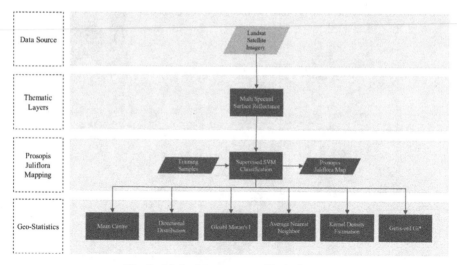

Fig. 2. Methodology process block diagram.

Two scenes of Landsat imagery footprint were required to cover full Sharjah city. The satellite images were collected during the dry season in UAE (August).

3.2 Thematic Layers Preparation

The Scan Line Corrector (SLC) of Landsat 7 failed On May 31, 2003. The sensor has acquired and delivered data with lined gap strips on each band [53]. For images obtained in 2010, nearest neighbor (NN) resampling was employed to fill the lined gap in each band. The closest input detector sample must be recognized and chosen as the output picture value for each output point. Figure 3 compares the image of Landsat 7 before and after Scan Line correction [52]. Both Landsat 7 and Landsat 8 were processed in the same way, using the same stages such as band stacking, scene mosaicking, and extracting the study region. For time series analysis, these steps are required. Figure 4 illustrates the main pre-processing steps common for all three satellite imagery.

3.3 Prosopis Juliflora Mapping

Using the spectral information from surface reflectance thematic layers, Prosopis Juliflora mapped using supervised classification. For classification, the Support Vector Machine Classifier was used. Using qualitative data of Prosopis Juliflora, two classes were defined based on the existence of Prosopis Juliflora as seen from satellite imagery, as well as information about probable additional land covers existing at each selected. One class represented by pure Prosopis Juliflora. Since Prosopis Juliflora invades agricultural regions, a new class for all other vegetation agriculture was created. In terms of spectral separability, both classes provide certain challenges. Prosopis Juliflora is polymorphic, and while it can be dominant or pure in some cases, it usually invades the habitat of other plants and so mixes with them in numerous forms, ranging from a shrub to a fully formed tree. As a result, this categorization only provides a very wide classification. As training samples, over 1000 pixel samples were gathered from each year. Training samples of Prosopis Juliflora was taken from the region below Sharjah Airport. With a total land area of roughly 21.19 km^2 and a latitude and longitude of (25° 20.614'N, 55° 31.639'E), the area is mostly vegetated with Prosopis Juliflora, which has medium canopy sizes (5–10 m diameters) and a variety of densities.

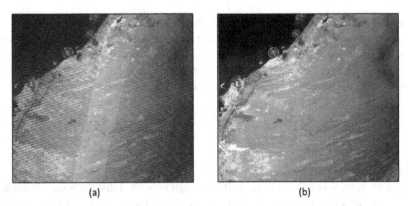

(a)   (b)

Fig. 3. Landsat 7 SLC correction Using Nearest Neighbor (NN) Resampling [52].

3.4 Geo-Statistics Modelling

Prosopis Juliflora maps were used to geographic statistical modelling first the geographic mean central and direction were found. After that, the recent Prosopis Juliflora map at year 2020 was used for further inductive analytics. This Moran I Spatial Autocorrelation were used to determine the spatial clustering patterns. Moreover, Nearest Neighbour Index and Kernel Density Estimation (KDE) were used to compute the observed and expected mean distances within the clusters, and the density of Prosopis Juliflora population over the observed area. Finally, statistical significance of high Prosopis Juliflora population values (hot spots) and low population values (cold spots) were identified by executing Getis-Ord Gi* hot spot analysis.

Measuring Spatial Clustering Using Moran I Spatial Autocorrelation
Moran's I is a measure to evaluate whether the spatial pattern is random, dispersed or clustered. The Moran's I Index creates a cross product between the Prosopis Juliflora count values and their spatial lag by measuring the mean and variance for each feature value, the deviation values for all neighbouring features are them multiplied together. The Moran's I Index is calculated in Eq. (1). Where zi is the deviation of the Prosopis Juliflora feature I from it mean, and So is the aggregate of all the spatial weights. The statistical significance is calculated by z-score and its associated p-value based on hypothesis test.

The possible scenarios are null hypothesis stating that Prosopis Juliflora are randomly disbursed, or alternate hypothesis that Prosopis Juliflora is more spatially clustered or dispersed

$$I = \frac{n}{S0} \frac{\sum_{i=1}^{n} \sum_{j=1}^{n} wizizj}{\sum_{i=1}^{n} zi^2} \tag{1}$$

Measuring Distances Between Clusters Using Nearest Neighbour'
The distances between each Prosopis Juliflora feature centroid and its nearest neighbour's centroid location is calculated by Average Nearest Neighbourhood Index by measuring the observed and expected mean distances within the clusters as Eq. 2. Where Do is the observed mean distance and De is expected mean distance

$$ANN = \frac{Do}{De} \tag{2}$$

Hot Spot Analysis Using Getis-Ord Gi*
Hot Spot analysis was utilized to pinpoint the regions with statistically significant high Prosopis Juliflora clustering or low Prosopis Juliflora. Getis-Ord Gi* Index was computed for each feature as Eq. 3 to determine the statistical significance z-scores and p-values.

$$Gi^* = \frac{\sum_{j=1}^{n} wi, jxj - \overline{X} \sum_{j=1}^{n} wi, j}{s\sqrt{\frac{n\sum_{j=1}^{n} w^2 i, j - (\sum_{i=1}^{n} wi, j)^2}{n-q}}} \tag{3}$$

4   Results and Discussion

The SVM supervised classification results showed an overall accuracy of 88% compared to visual ground samples collected manually from Google Earth Maps. The support Vector Machine's multi-temporal analysis of the vegetated areas of Prosopis Juliflora trees in Sharjah for the years 2000, 2010, and 2020 revealed that the maximum density appeared in 2020 with 14.13 km^2, followed by year 2000 with a total area of 11.99 km^2. Finally, with 9.26km^2 of total vegetated land in 2010, 2010 was the year with the least total vegetated area. Figure 4 maps Prosopis Juliflora areas in Sharjah city in year 2000, 2010 and 2020 [52] (Table 2).

Table 2. Accuracy Assessment of SVM classification.

Kappa	TP Rate	TN Rate	Precision	Recall	OA Accuracy
0.7303	0.723	0.031	0.922	0.723	88.57%

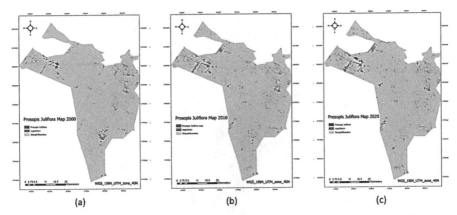

Fig. 4. Total Prosopis Juliflora in Sharjah City in (a) 2000, (b) 2010, (c) 2020 [52].

The geographical mean and directional distribution of Prosopis Juliflora distribution over 2000, 2010 and 2020 showed that in 2000, the mean canter was located at 25.19991°N, 55.69553°E, in 2010 the mean canter was shifted 8 km to the north at 25.25823°N, 55.64063°E. in 2020, the mean centre was shifted from 2010 to the east by 8.9 Km² at 25.33809°N, 55.64692°E. The directional trend within the total displacement from 2000 to 2020 was around 16 Km² in the direction of north-east toward the eastern boarders of the city. Quantitively, the total area of Prosopis Juliflora vegetation cover increased from 12 Km² in 2020 to 14.13 Km². Figure 5 shows the geographical mean and directional distribution of Prosopis Juliflora distribution.

The null hypothesis is rejected after Moran I statistical significance test revealed that the p-value is statistically significant and the z-score is positive. The probability of this clustered pattern being the result of random chance is less than 5%. As a result, Prosopis Juliflora's spatial distribution is more spatially clustered than would be predicted if the underlying spatial processes were random. Table 3 and Fig. 6 shows Moran I statistics significance test.

The Nearest Neighbour Index measured for Prosopis Juliflora and valued 0.111030, suggests that the observed mean distance between the clusters is 30.9 m. Figure 7 illustrate the statistical significance of Prosopis Juliflora Nearest Neighbour Index. Further analysis of Prosopis Juliflora invasion pattern is carried by Kernel Density Estimation. The average density was measured at around 300 trees/Km² located at 25.32358°N, 55.5601924°E. it is also observed that most of the trees are dense in the eastern boarders of the city.

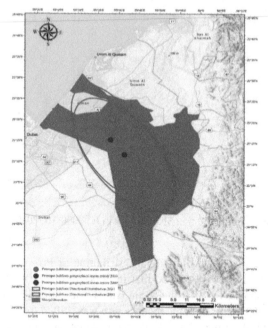

Fig. 5. Geographical mean and directional distribution of Prosopis Juliflora distribution over 2000, 2010 and 2020.

Table 3. Moran I statistics significance test.

Moran's Index	Variance	Z-score	P-value
0.102455	0.003618	2.239572	0.025119

Finally, Hot spots were found emerging the eastern side of the city, indicating high tree density of Prosopis Juliflora communities with more than 50 trees per community. The highest hotspot were found with around 3000 tree per community spatially clustered together. On the other hand, cold spots were found more the southern portion of the city with less than 50 trees per community. Figure 8 shows hot and cold spots of Prosopis Juliflora.

With a stand density of 500–1000 trees/ha, a secondary selective thinning is required to achieve the ideal final density of 100–625 trees/ha or less, spaced 5–10 m apart. The ANN Index, KDE and hotspot analysis, suggest that most Prosopis Juliflora is still under controllable secondary scheme in the eastern and southern part of the city, except of some areas in the eastern and western part of the city requires thinning.

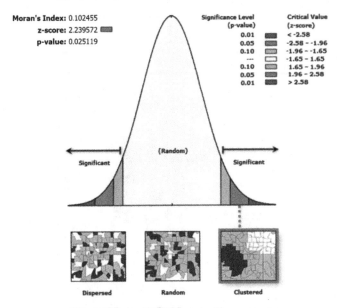

Fig. 6. Moran I statistical significance test.

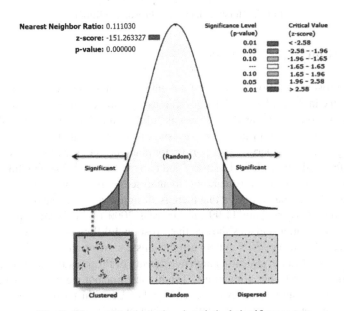

Fig. 7. Nearest Neighbourhood statistical significance test.

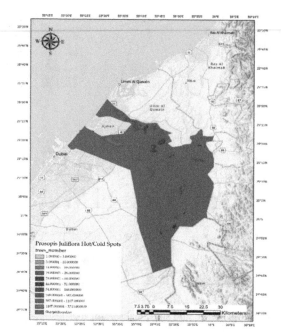

Fig. 8. Hotspot analysis of Prosopis juliflora.

5 Conclusion

Identifying Prosopis Juliflora sites is a vital environmental and ecological endeavour for any country in the arid zone. An algorithm using remote sensing data and GIS was created in this work to find areas of Prosopis Juliflora and its statistics distribution in Sharjah, UAE. The algorithm stated over two stages covering year 2000, 2010, and 2020. The first stage is to use supervised support vector machine classification to process multi spectral surface reflectance from Landsat 7 and 8 to map areas of Prosopis Juliflora. The second stage is to use Geo-statistical tools to analyse the tree's spatial distributions.

Prosopis Juliflora maps showed that there is an significant increase of the total cover by 1.17% over 20 years from 11.99 km^2 in year 2000 to 14.13 km^2 in year 2020. Furthermore, the spatial statistics showed that Prosopis Juliflora is spatial clustered with observed mean distance of 30.9 m between the clusters. Most clusters where emerging the eastern side of the city, indicating high tree density of Prosopis Juliflora communities with more than 50 trees per community. The highest hotspot were found with around 3000 tree per community spatially clustered together. Less clustering were found more in the southern portion of the city with less than 50 trees per community. Figure 8 shows hot and cold spots of Prosopis Juliflora. This conclude that a secondary selective thinning is required in Sharjah city to stop to invasion pf Prosopis Juliflora to achieve the ideal final density of 100–625 trees/ha or less, spaced 5–10 m apart. The ANN Index, KDE and hotspot analysis, suggest that most Prosopis Juliflora is still under controllable secondary scheme in the eastern and southern part of the city, except of some areas in the eastern and western part of the city requires thinning.

References

1. Essl, F., et al.: Which taxa are alien? criteria, applications, and uncertainties. BioScience **68**(7) (2018). https://doi.org/10.1093/biosci/biy057
2. Colautti, R.I., MacIsaac, H.I.: A neutral terminology to define 'invasive' species. Divers. Distrib. **10**(2) (2004). https://doi.org/10.1111/j.1366-9516.2004.00061.x
3. Levin, L.A., Crooks, J.A.: Functional consequences of invasive species in coastal and estuarine systems. In: Treatise on Estuarine and Coastal Science, vol. 7 (2012)
4. Groves, R.H.: Plant invasions of Australia: an overview. Ecol. Biol. Invasions (1986)
5. Charles, H., Dukes, J.S.: Impacts of invasive species on ecosystem services. In: Biological Invasions (2007)
6. Thomaz, S.M., Kovalenko, K.E., Havel, J.E., Kats, L.B.: Aquatic invasive species: general trends in the literature and introduction to the special issue. Hydrobiologia **746**(1) (2015). https://doi.org/10.1007/s10750-014-2150-8
7. Hulme, P.E.: Invasive species challenge the global response to emerging diseases. Trends Parasitol. **30**(6) (2014). https://doi.org/10.1016/j.pt.2014.03.005
8. Wallace, R.D., Bargeron, C.T., Reaser, J.K.: Enabling decisions that make a difference: guidance for improving access to and analysis of invasive species information. Biol. Invas. **22**(1) (2020). https://doi.org/10.1007/s10530-019-02142-2
9. Perrings, C., Burgiel, S., Lonsdale, M., Mooney, H., Williamson, M.: International cooperation in the solution to trade-related invasive species risks. Ann. N. Y. Acad, Sci. **1195** (2010). https://doi.org/10.1111/j.1749-6632.2010.05453.x
10. HDRA: Identifying tropical Prosopis species: a field guide. Coventry, UK (2003). ISBN:0-905343-34-4
11. Dubow, J.: Still-life, after-life, nature morte, W.G. Sebald and the demands of landscape. In: Envisioning Landscapes, Making Worlds Geography and the Humanities (2012)
12. Patnaik, P., Abbasi, T., Abbasi, S.A.: Prosopis (Prosopis juliflora): Blessing and bane. Trop. Ecol. **58**(3) (2017)
13. de Ataide Silva, M.: Botany, taxonomy and distribution of the Genus Prosopis L. In: Habit, M.A., Saavedra, J.C. (eds.) The Current State of Knowledge on Prosopis Juliflora, Rome (1988)
14. Burkart, A.: A Monograph of The Genus Prosopis (Leguminosae Subfam. Mimosoideae). J. Arnold Arbor. **57**(3) (1976)
15. Ashton, M.S., Gunatilleke, S., De Zoysa, N., Dassanayake, M.D., Gunatilleke, N., Wijesundera, S.: A Field Guide to the Common Trees and Shrubs of Sri Lanka, vol. 7, no. November 2011 (1997)
16. Yoda, K., Hoshino, B., Nawata, H., Yasuda, H.: Root system development of Prosopis Deedlings under different soil moisture conditions. 沙漠研究 日本沙漠学会誌age Removed] **22**(1) (2012)
17. Muturi, G.M., Poorter, L., Bala, P., Mohren, G.M.J.: Unleached Prosopis litter inhibits germination but leached stimulates seedling growth of dry woodland species. J. Arid Environ. **138** (2017). https://doi.org/10.1016/j.jaridenv.2016.12.003
18. Abbasi, T., Abbasi, S.A.: Sources of pollution in rooftop rainwater harvesting systems and their control. Crit. Rev. Environ. Sci. Technol. **41**(23) (2011). https://doi.org/10.1080/106 43389.2010.497438
19. Warrag, M.O.A.: Autotoxic potential of foliage on seed germination and early growth of mesquite (Prosopis juliflora). J. Arid Environ. **31**(4) (1995). https://doi.org/10.1016/S0140-1963(05)80124-7
20. Warrag, M.O.A.: Autotoxicity of mesquite (Prosopis juliflora) pericarps on seed germination and seedling growth. J. Arid Environ. **27**(1) (1994). https://doi.org/10.1006/jare.1994.1047

21. Gunarathne, R.M.U.K., Perera, G.A.D.: Does the invasion of Prosopis juliflora cause the die-back of the native Manilkara hexandra in seasonally dry tropical forests of Sri Lanka? Trop. Ecol. **57**(3), 475–488 (2016)

22. Naudiyal, N., Schmerbeck, J., Gärtner, S.: What influences the plant community composition on Delhi ridge? The role played by Prosopis juliflora and anthropogenic disturbances. Trop. Ecol. **58**(1) (2017)

23. Mwangi, E., Swallow, B.: Invasion of Prosopis Juliflora and local livelihoods. Case study of Lake Baringo area of Kenya (2005)

24. Ahlawat, M., Dahiya, P., Chaudhary, D.: Allergenic pollen in the atmosphere of Rohtak city, Haryana (India): apioneer study. Aerobiologia (Bologna). **30**(3) (2014). https://doi.org/10.1007/s10453-013-9323-1

25. George, S., Manoharan, D., Li, J., Britton, M., Parida, A.: Transcriptomic responses to drought and salt stress in desert tree Prosopis Juliflora. Plant Gene **12** (2017). https://doi.org/10.1016/j.plgene.2017.09.004

26. Kim, S.H., Park, H.S., Jang, J.Y.: Impact of meteorological variation on hospital visits of patients with tree pollen allergy. BMC Public Health **11** (2011). https://doi.org/10.1186/1471-2458-11-890

27. Hussain, M.I., Shackleton, R.T., El-Keblawy, A., Del Mar Trigo Pérez, M. and González, L.: Invasive mesquite (Prosopis Juliflora), an allergy and health challenge. Plants **9**(2) (2020). https://doi.org/10.3390/plants9020141

28. Tessema, Y.: Ecological and economic dimensions of the paradoxical invasive species-Prosopis juliflora and policy challenges in Ethiopia. J. Econ. Sustain. Dev. **3**(8) (2012)

29. Haji, J., Mohammed, A.: Economic impact of Prosopis Juliflora on agropastoral households of Dire Dawa Administration, Ethiopia. Af. J. Agric. **8**(9), 768–779 (2013). https://doi.org/10.5897/AJAR12.014

30. Edrisi, S.A., El-Keblawy, A., Abhilash, P.C.: Sustainability analysis of Prosopis Juliflora (Sw.) DC based restoration of degraded land in North India. Land **9**(2) (2020). https://doi.org/10.3390/land9020059

31. Hussain, M.I., Shackleton, R.T., El-Keblawy, A., Del Mar Trigo Pérez, M., González, L.: Comparison of survey methods for an invasive plant at the subwatershed level. Biol. Invas. **7**(3) (2005). https://doi.org/10.1007/s10530-004-3904-4

32. Joshi, N., et al.: A review of the application of optical and radar remote sensing data fusion to land use mapping and monitoring. Remote Sens. **8**(1) (2016). https://doi.org/10.3390/rs8010070

33. Sakachep, Z.K., Rai, P.K.: Influence of invasive alien plants on vegetation of Hailakandi district, Assam, north-east, India. Indian J. Ecol. **48**(1) (2021)

34. Pandit, R., Laband, D.N.: Spatial autocorrelation in country-level models of species imperilment. Ecol. Econ. **60**(3) (2007). https://doi.org/10.1016/j.ecolecon.2006.07.018

35. Dark, S.J.: The biogeography of invasive alien plants in California: An application of GIS and spatial regression analysis. Divers. Distrib. **10**(1) (2004). https://doi.org/10.1111/j.1472-4642.2004.00054.x

36. Siesa, M.E., Manenti, R., Padoa-Schioppa, E., De Bernardi, F., Ficetola, G.F.: Spatial auto-correlation and the analysis of invasion processes from distribution data: A study with the crayfish Procambarus clarkia. Biol. Invas. **13**(9) (2011). https://doi.org/10.1007/s10530-011-0032-9

37. Christen, D.C., Matlack, G.R.: The habitat and conduit functions of roads in the spread of three invasive plant species. Biol. Invas. **11**(2) (2009). https://doi.org/10.1007/s10530-008-9262-x

38. Kazmi, J.H., Haase, D., Shahzad, A., Shaikh, S., Zaidi, S.M., Qureshi, S.: Mapping spatial distribution of invasive alien species through satellite remote sensing in Karachi, Pakistan: an

urban ecological perspective. Int. J. Environ. Sci. Technol. (2021). https://doi.org/10.1007/s13762-021-03304-3

39. Mbaabu, P.R., et al.: Spatial evolution of prosopis invasion and its effects on LULC and livelihoods in Baringo, Kenya. Remote Sens. **11**(10) (2019). https://doi.org/10.3390/rs1110 1217

40. Vidhya, R., Vijayasekaran, D., Ramakrishnan, S.S.: Mapping invasive plant Prosopis juliflora in arid land using high resolution remote sensing data and biophysical parameters. Ind. J. Geo-Marine Sci. **46**(6) (2017)

41. Meroni, M., et al.: Mapping Prosopis juliflora in West Somaliland with Landsat 8 satellite imagery and ground information. L. Degrad. Dev. **28**(2) (2017). https://doi.org/10.1002/ldr. 2611

42. Rembold, F., Leonardi, U., Ng, W.T., Gadain, H., Meroni, M., Atzberger, C.: Mapping areas invaded by Prosopisjuliflora in Somaliland on Landsat 8 imagery. In: Remote Sensing for Agriculture, Ecosystems, and Hydrology XVII, vol. 9637 (2015). https://doi.org/10.1117/12. 2193133

43. Ragavan, K., Johnny, J.C.: Quantification of Invasive Colonies of Prosopis Juliflora Using Remote Sensing and GIS Techniques. (5), 110–115 (2015). www.erpublication.org

44. Issa, S., Dohai, B.: Gis Analysis of invasive Prosopis Juliflora dynamics in two selected sites From the United Arab Emirates. Can. J. Pure Appl. Sci. **2**(1), 235–242 (2008). http://www. cjpas.net/Jan-08.pdf#page=121

45. Wakie, T.T., Evangelista, P.H., Jarnevich, C.S., Laituri, M.: Mapping current and potential distribution of non-native Prosopis Juliflorain the Afar region of Ethiopia. PLoS One **9**(11) (2014). https://doi.org/10.1371/journal.pone.0112854

46. Hoshino, B., et al.: Remote sensing methods for the evaluation of the mesquite tree (Prosopis juliflora) environmental adaptation to semi-arid Africa (2011). https://doi.org/10.1109/IGA RSS.2011.6049498

47. Reddy, C.S.: Applications of GIS in plant taxonomy, species distribution and ecology. J. Econ. Taxon. Bot. **41**(3–4) (2017)

48. O'Donnell, J., Gallagher, R.V., Wilson, P.D., Downey, P.O., Hughes, L., Leishman, M.R.: Invasion hotspots for non-native plants in Australia under current and future climates. Glob. Change Biol. **18**(2) (2012). https://doi.org/10.1111/j.1365-2486.2011.02537.x

49. O'Neill, M.W., Bradley, B.A., Allen, J.M.: Hotspots of invasive plant abundance are geographically distinct from hotspots of establishment. Biol. Invas. **23**(4) (2021). https://doi.org/10.1007/s10530-020-02433-z

50. Böer, B.: An introduction to the climate of the United Arab Emirates. J. Arid Environ. **35**(1) (1997). https://doi.org/10.1006/jare.1996.0162

51. Sherif, M., Chowdhury, R., Shetty, A.: Rainfall and Intensity-Duration-Frequency (IDF) Curves in the United Arab Emirates (2014). https://doi.org/10.1061/9780784413548.231

52. AlMaazmi, A., Al-Ruzouq, R.: Multitemporal remote sensing for invasive Prosopis Juliflora plants mapping and monitoring: Sharjah, UAE (2021). https://doi.org/10.5220/001044060 1490156

53. Landsat Missions: Landsat 7 Scan Line Corrector Processing Algorithm Theoretical Basis (2003). https://www.usgs.gov/media/files/landsat-7-scan-line-corrector-processing-alg orithm-theoretical-basis

Progress on Land Surface Phenology Estimation with Multispectral Remote Sensing

Irini Soubry[1]([✉]) [iD], Ioannis Manakos[2] [iD], and Chariton Kalaitzidis[3] [iD]

[1] Department of Geography and Planning, University of Saskatchewan, Saskatoon,
SK S7N5C8, Canada
`irini.soubry@usask.ca`
[2] Information Technologies Institute, Centre for Research and Technology Hellas,
57001 Thessaloniki, Greece
`imanakos@iti.gr`
[3] Department of Geoinformation in Environmental Management, Institute of Chania,
Mediterranean Agronomic, 73100 Crete, Greece
`chariton@maich.gr`

Abstract. Phenological information can shed more light on the spatiotemporal biological processes that occur in vegetation communities. It facilitates ecosystem and resources management, conservation, restoration, policy and decision-making on local, national, and global scales. Vegetation phenology relates, among others, to the seasonal growth stages of flowering and leaf fall of specific species on the ground and is different from Land Surface Phenology (LSP), which looks at the spatiotemporal vegetation development of the land surface as measured by satellite sensors. There is a wide range of Earth Observation datasets and methods to estimate LSP. This paper reviews current progress in LSP estimation with multispectral sensing for natural and semi natural environments. It includes the satellite sensors' capacity to capture LSP, data fusion techniques, synergies, and cloud computing, machine learning, and data cube processing. One section is dedicated to the validation of LSP products and its challenges. Lastly, a short review on existing ground phenology networks, open-source software tools, and global LSP products is provided.

Keywords: Land surface phenology · Multi-source data fusion · Time series analysis · Phenology metrics · Phenology validation · Phenology networks · Global phenology products

1 Introduction

Plant and animal growth cycles are changing continuously in response to their environment. Quantitative evidence about the pulsing of the vegetation cover over terrestrial biomes provides an insight about climate change, desertification, or land use changes. Vegetation phenology refers to the changes in seasonal patterns of natural phenomena on the land, e.g. leaf out, flowering, leaf browning and fall, influenced by annual and seasonal fluctuations of biotic and abiotic (e.g. temperature, day length, precipitation)

C. Grueau et al. (Eds.): GISTAM 2021/2022, CCIS 1908, pp. 16–37, 2023.
https://doi.org/10.1007/978-3-031-44112-7_2

drivers [1, 2]. Plant phenology is controlling net primary productivity, as well as seasonal fluxes of water, energy, and CO_2 between land and atmosphere [3].

On a regional level, agencies and organizations need phenology information to evaluate their conservation goals, and to conduct assessments related to the vulnerability and the potential adaptation of the region. On a national scale, phenology dates are helpful to the environmental protection agencies, as indicators of seasonal weather change impacts. Lastly, if the trend related to the impact of seasonal weather changes on specific phenology cycle metrics is significant on a global level, atmospheric scientists and the Intergovernmental Panel on Climate Change could consider season length or seasonal photosynthesis as contributing information in understanding atmospheric circulation patterns [4].

The main drivers of vegetation phenology are related to climate and vary across ecoregions [5]. In temperate regions like Central Europe, temperature is the main driver [6, 7]. In dry and semi-dry climates, water availability, soil moisture and precipitation [8] are of major importance [7, 10, 11]. This paper reviews phenology monitoring in natural and semi-natural vegetation. By semi-natural vegetation, one means vegetation that includes "extensively managed grasslands, agro-forestry areas and all vegetated features that are not used for crop production" [11]. Specifically, this paper looks at the study of Land Surface Phenology (LSP), which is the study of the spatiotemporal vegetation development of the land surface as measured by satellite sensors, and is different from species-specific phenology observed on the ground [12, 13]. LSP represents the aggregated dynamics of multiple individual organisms in every remote sensing pixel, mixed with other land covers; therefore, it is considered essentially distinct to *in situ* measurements of single organisms [14, 15].

LSP science has developed immensely in the last two decades. Past reviews tackle LSP methods and their limitations [32, 33], LSP products [34, 35], phenology networks [35, 36], and challenges that arise in LSP of optical remote sensing [35–38] separately. This review reports the recent advances and future trends for LSP retrieval of natural and semi-natural vegetation with multispectral sensors. A shorter version was published in the proceedings of the 7th International Conference on Geographical Information Systems Theory, Applications and Management [38]. This version provides more detail on the state of the art of LSP estimation, including multispectral sensors, data fusion, synergies, software tools, products, and networks. It also adds an important section related to the validation of LSP products.

2 Current Sensor Advances

Phenology cycles can be approximated from spaceborne time series of vegetation indices (VIs) [9]. Remote sensing, "the acquisition of information about the state and condition of an object through sensors that do not touch it" [16], is used for that goal. Over the years, global spaceborne phenology products based on LSP have been developed [18–21] through remote sensors that can approximate LSP. LiDAR [21], SAR [22, 23], passive microwave remote sensing [24, 25], and fluorescence remote sensing systems [26] have been used for LSP estimation. However, the use of multispectral remote sensing is more common because different phenological stages can be detected with multispectral sensors from changes in vegetation pigments. Here, we focus on current and future multispectral remote sensing missions for LSP estimation (Table 1).

AVHRR has been used to study vegetation fluxes [10] and LSP trends [15]. Improvements to its coarse spatial resolution (1.1 to 8 km) came with MODIS, which is still being used to assess spatio-temporal LSP patterns [39, 40]. The VIIRS LSP product follows-up the MODIS product, and is being used for global LSP estimation [41, 42].

LSP can also be estimated from geostationary satellites, such as the SEVIRI sensor, which has been used to assess LSP in the studies of [54] and [55]. Recent studies used AHI on the geostationary Himawari-8 satellite to estimate LSP over the Asian-Pacific region [57, 59], and to study the sun-angle effects on LSP [58].

When looking at moderate resolution multispectral sensors, Landsat facilitates the identification of regional alterations caused by the abundance of various plant species [61] and the registration of LSP variations set by micro-climatic and topographic effects. The heterogeneity in land cover classes within each pixel is low, allowing for better field matching. Landsat's 40-year continuity currently gives room for large opportunities in LSP time series development when combined with cloud-computing and machine learning in image processing (see Sect. 5.1). The recent launch of Landsat 9 on 27 September of 2021 and initial thoughts on Landsat 10 including new imaging technologies, international collaborations, and inclusion of the commercial sector, will preserve data continuity [82].

The spatio-temporal resolution of Landsat is in many cases still too coarse for fine scale LSP estimation. Therefore, new approaches of satellite constellations are employed to increase these resolutions. The Sentinel-2 MultiSpectral Instrument (MSI) improves the temporal and spatial coverage of Landsat and is used for LSP extraction [67, 68]. Sentinel-2 and Landsat data complement each other, enabling integration [83]. They generate an average temporal overpass of 2.9 days [84], maximizing the chances of cloud-free surface data for LSP estimation.

Very high spatial (<10 m) and temporal resolution data from commercial satellite sensors can improve LSP estimation even more. PlanetScope was used for phenology estimation in semi-arid rangelands and showed promising results [71]. Most of its applications for phenology monitoring are related to agriculture [73, 74]. VENμS has also been used for LSP studies related to crop phenology, such as the optimization of crop emergence estimation [78], or the simulation of its bands for maize yield estimation through phenology [79]. Transformation functions between Sentinel-2 and VENμS surface reflectance allow for their combination into one dense time-series for vegetation monitoring [80]. Nevertheless, VENμS only covers selected sites on the globe [85].

New satellite sensors scheduled to launch will support LSP monitoring. The JPSS mission, that carries the VIIRS instrument, will launch three spacecrafts between 2021 and 2031 [86]. Meanwhile, the Planetscope nanosatellite constellation is launching continuously every three to six months. In the end, this will result in daily images of the entire globe at very high spatial resolution (3m approximately) [87].

Table 1. Satellite sensor characteristics for LSP (Land Surface Phenology) studies and example applications. Source: [38].

Satellite sensor	Orbit-type	Operation timespan	Spatial resolution	Temporal resolution	Example LSP applications	Relevant studies	Data Source
AVHRR	Sun-synchronous	1978-Present	1.1 km at nadir	Daily	global LSP trends;	[11, 16, 44]	[44]
MODIS	Sun-synchronous	1999-Present	250 m, 500 m, 1 km	Daily	global LSP trends;	[3, 15, 35, 40, 41, 46–50]	[50]
VIIRS	Sun-synchronous	2011-Present	375 m, 250m, 750 m	Daily	global LSP trends, comparison of global products, comparison with ground phenology;	[42, 43, 52, 53]	[53]
SEVIRI	Geostationary	2002-Present	1 km, 3 km	15 min	regional LSP trends;	[54, 55]	[56]
AHI	Geostationary	2014-Present	500 m, 1 km, 2 km	10 min	regional LSP trends;	[58–60]	[60]
Landsat	Sun-synchronous	1972-Present	30 m, 80 m	16-days, 18-days	LSP trends, comparison with ground phenology, land cover characterization;	[62–65]	[65]
Sentinel-2	Sun-synchronous	2015-Present	10 m, 20 m, 60 m	5-days, 10-days	LSP trends, comparison with ground phenology;	[67–70]	[70]
PlanetScope	Sun-synchronous	2009-Present	3.7 m at nadir	Daily	LSP trends in agriculture;	[72–75]	[76–78]
VENμS	Sun-synchronous	2017-Present	3 m, 5.3 m	2-days	LSP trends in agriculture;	[79–81]	[81]

3 LSP Estimation Using Multi-Source Earth Observation

A composite cloud-free image utilizes cloud-free parts of images of close dates [89]. These type of images are produced from AVHRR, MODIS, and SPOT data to account for cloud cover. One drawback of this method is that the temporal frequency of the data, required for LSP, is lower. On the other hand, data fusion or blending of satellite data from different sensors can generate synthetic information of high spatiotemporal resolution [90]. Also, synergies between satellite products, such as Sentinel-2 and Landsat-8 can be used to densify time series. In this case, each product of the synergy remains unchanged. Data fusion and synergies facilitate LSP estimations with their high temporal and spatial resolution, allowing for detailed phenology cycles. Examples of recent data integration methods are included in Table 2.

Efforts have been made to extract medium resolution (MR) (10–100 m) LSP metrics through various data fusion methods. FORCE ImproPhe allows for the prediction of MR LSP based on corresponding coarse resolution (0.1–2 km) LSP [91]. Information from the local pixel neighborhood from both sources is obtained, and spectral distance and multiscale heterogeneity metrics are used as predictor variables. Another approach

Table 2. Examples of satellite data integration methods (i.e. data fusion and synergies). Adapted from [38].

Data integration method	Satellite sensor combinations	Details	Source
FORCE ImproPhe	MODIS, Landsat, Sentinel	Uses local pixel neighborhood, denoises LSP, preserves sharp edges	[92–94]
Multi-year high resolution data composition	Landsat	Accounts for higher spatial heterogeneity	[94]
Automatic co-registration	Landsat, Sentinel	Co-registration of Landsat-8 to Sentinel-2A & Sentinel-2A to Sentinel-2B	[95]
Assisted downscaling	Landsat, Sentinel	Downscales Landsat-8 to Sentinel-2 resolution	[84]
Super-resolution enhancement	Landsat, Sentinel	Uses convolution neural networks trained with Sentinel-2 data	[29]
HLS	Landsat, Sentinel	A combined Landsat/Sentinel product	[96, 97]

synthesizes multiple years of medium resolution data into a single LSP curve. This method was used with a 32-year Landsat time series to define the growing season in the forests of the Northern Hemisphere [94]. Nijland et al. [98] used the same approach to extract average yearly LSP curves in mixed stands and conifer forests of Rocky Mountains (CA) from 1984 to 2014.

Other studies that address vegetation seasonality evaluate the juxtaposition of Sentinel-2 and Landsat-8 products [99, 100]. Due to differences between the two sensors, cross-calibration is needed for their integration, such as automatic co-registration [95], assisted downscaling [28], and super-resolution enhancement [29]. In these studies, the replacement of the NIR band with the first red-edge Sentinel-2 band has shown to provide better comparisons with Landsat data, since its range is more similar to the Landsat NIR band [101, 102].

Lastly, a synergy between Landsat 8 and Sentinel-2 was developed through the Multi-source Land Imaging (MuSLI) program of NASA [101]. This product is the Harmonized Landsat Sentinel-2 (HLS) dataset. It is a global product that provides land surface observations every 2 to 3 days at 30 m spatial resolution [103], and has been used for the development of an operational LSP product [104]. The combination of these satellite sensors generates time series with unprecedented frequency. However, one should be aware of the various theoretical and technical hurdles when using different sensor constellations.

4 Validation of LSP Products

Multiple satellite missions and new image processing technologies arose in recent years, allowing for higher spatial and temporal resolution of data individually, or through fusions and synergies [28–30]. Moving to a finer scale helps unfold local structures associated with microclimate, species distribution and composition, disturbance factors, and land utilization. Nevertheless, phenological ground observations are required to validate the results obtained from spaceborne products' estimations [30]. Validation of LSP results encompasses many challenges and still remains an active research topic [31, 32].

Plot scale phenology usually measures individual species. LSP observations are maximum value composites with a regular observation interval derived from a specific observation period, generated from irregular observation intervals collected from satellite remote sensing. In several studies the LSP changes that were observed through remote sensing were greater than the ones in ground phenology data [3, 32, 41, 47]. The seasonal patterns detected from Earth observation data cannot be linked 1:1 to actual differences in vegetation phenology [32], and their accuracy could vary between ecosystems [105]. To link LSP estimations with ground phenology observations one should understand the species composition in the study area [48]. Simultaneous field-based and RS data are needed along different stages of multiple growing seasons [14]. After this, up-scaling can be done by combining field observations with a high-resolution satellite image, to produce a higher resolution map of the field parameter that was observed. This map can then be compared to the medium resolution satellite data [106]. Overall, it is important for users to be aware of the data product limitations, so as not to be led to inaccurate and misleading phenology monitoring.

4.1 Ground Phenology Monitoring

Detailed ground phenology information is most commonly acquired as point measurements in random spatial patterns, and phenological stages are registered in standardized numeric codes [107]. The main downside of plot scale phenological data is that it is time- and resource-consuming, localized, and observes a small sample of species [48]. Therefore, several countries use crowd-sourcing to obtain such information. Current methods used for the retrieval of ground phenology data include:

- phenology diary reports of ground observation sites; for example, the USA National Phenology Network (USA-NPN) created the National Phenology Database (NPDb) that contains data collected from scientists and trained volunteers; it is comprised of field-based observations of plants and animals [4]); also the BBCH (Biologische Bundesanstalt, Bundessortenamt und CHemische Industrie) scale is a uniform coding system (from 0 to 10) of phenologically similar growth stages among plants that is being used for ground phenology monitoring [108, 109];
- optical phenology towers to generate vegetation greenness indices close to the surface with high temporal resolution [31, 105]; these towers have in most cases ground-based visible spectrum digital cameras to monitor vegetation development with repeating photography during the growing season [64, 98];

- ground radiometric measurements with a handheld radiometer of crop canopies during the growing season to define a semi-empirical model for the time profile of the vegetation index for each crop at the regional scale [47, 110];
- gross primary production (GPP) retrieved from a flux tower observation network [3, 110];
- air temperature records [105].

Recently, improved alternative ground-based LSP validation methods are being used at ground networks around the globe. Examples include ground-based phenological cameras, *in situ* forest canopy greenness indices from phenology towers, and flux-measured GPP. The Society of Biometeorology Phenology Commission (ISB-PC) and the World Meteorological Organization Commission for Agricultural Meteorology (WMO-CAgM) built a Global Alliance of Phenological Observation Networks (GAPON) [2]. The phenology networks in this community are up to date 53 in number, and include –among others- nationwide approaches. Examples of large phenological networks are provided in Table 3.

4.2 Ground Reference vs. Ground Truth Data

Ground phenological observations differ from estimations of biophysical parameters, such as ground spectral measurements or LSP, and are mostly related to the subjective decision of the data collector. Different individuals can give different phenology dates for the same sampling site and, as a result, ground data collection relies heavily on the collector's experience and knowledge. However, precise instructions, such as the use of the BBCH scales [108] with photo examples could help the observer. Nevertheless, it is not so straightforward to select a derived LSP method, which will match precisely with ground phenology (GP) data. In reality, collecting extensive *in situ* measurements at the same frequency of LSP data is problematic for common small research teams consisting of a few scientists and students [14].

Moreover, according to Rankine et al. [31], simultaneous multi-annual observations of vegetation greenness from satellite and near-surface observations are not so common due to the challenges that exist in relation to implementing and maintaining sensitive radiometric instrumentation. They believe that another factor that limits direct comparisons between GP and LSP is the spectral bands adopted to construct the VI. Narrowband and broadband vegetation indices have different sensitivity to alterations in leaf area and chlorophyll content.

Another issue is the way in which the Start of Season (SOS) is defined. This can be different, depending on the method used for LSP extraction [34]. The results of Wu et al. [46] showed that the modelled SOS outputs tend to appear on earlier dates than the ground observations, irrespective of the method used to model the metric. This is also consistent with the scaling study of Zhang et al. [115], where the earlier SOS pixels define the SOS detection at coarse resolution more than the later SOS pixels of an area. Interestingly, it has been found that SOS at coarser resolution (i.e. 500 m), corresponds to vegetation green up of 30% of the total pixel area, despite the variation in SOS dates within [115]. One reason could be that different LSP-SOS metrics represent different ground phenology-SOS observations [48]. Similar difficulties arise when trying

Table 3. Major existing phenology networks. Information retrieved from GLOBE [20], Nasahara & Nagai [111], NEON [18], PEN [112], PEP725 [19], Templ et al. [113], USA-NPN [17], PHENOCAM [114]. Source [38].

Phenology Networks	Purpose	Users	Collaborations	Extra information
USA-NPN	Collect, store, distribute phenology data	Researchers, natural resource managers, policy-makers, educators, citizen scientists, NGO's	-NEON; -Nature's Notebook	Standardized plant & animal observation protocols
NEON	Collect ecological data: *in situ* measurements/ observations & airborne remote sensing surveys	Researchers	-81 field sites in US	175 open access products
PEP725	Open access database to facilitate phenological research, education, environmental monitoring	Researchers, educators	-7 phenology network partners; -32 European meteorological services	-Volunteer data collected from 1868 to present; -12 million records
GLOBE	International science and education program to promote teaching and learning of science	Students, educators	-NASA, NSF, NOAA; -121 countries	Over 150 million ground biophysical measurements
PEN	Validate terrestrial RS products of ecology, phenology changes	Ecologists, remote sensing specialists, scientists, citizens	-FluxNet, ILTER, AsiaFlux -38 sites worldwide, most in Japan	Some sites measure environmental ecophysiological properties
PhenoCam	For phenological model validation, evaluation of satellite RS products, studies of climate change impacts on terrestrial ecosystems	Researchers, remote sensing specialists	-750 sites across North America	Data derived from visible-wavelength digital camera imagery

to define the End of Season (EOS). This is because plant canopy greenness changes gradually in autumn. EOS estimation becomes even harder for evergreen species, for which the greenness changes only slightly [131]. Therefore, small differences of EOS between years are even more difficult to detect accurately using remote sensing data [46]. Therefore, it is important to implement standardized protocols for ground phenology monitoring [116], as well as for LSP metrics extraction. An effort towards that direction, as far as ground phenology monitoring is concerned, has resulted in the plant phenology monitoring design of NEON [117]. Unfortunately this has not yet been implemented with consistency around the globe [117], which is why studies that integrate field-based validation vary [31, 98].

4.3 Spatial Cross-Scale Issues

While being very valuable, field measurements often represent a small area and are in most cases subjective, because of the approach being used [98]. Up until now it has not been an easy task to match field and satellite-based observations because of the difficulty to transpose these measurements to the same scale and because of the use of phenological metrics that are approximations of the phenophases [106]. The spatial mismatch between the field-based point measurements of plots and the resolution of satellite pixels at local scales, particularly medium resolution data, further complicates the process [61]. This happens because most field data are usually species-specific and observed at scales that are incompatible with medium resolution remote sensing observations.

More specifically, this relates to the issue of scale mismatch due to vegetation heterogeneity [118]. It is rare for vegetation to be uniform in the Landsat or Sentinel-2 resolution, whereas in field observations, budburst or flowering stages are identified for a small amount of plants in each sampling plot. Thus, relating *in situ* phenological events with the mean LSP of a Landsat or Sentinel-2 pixel is difficult, as these pixels are spectrally mixed [31]. Furthermore, in cases of mixed pixels containing vegetated and non-vegetated areas, the interpretation of the LSP metrics' biophysical meaning could be misleading. In these cases, the LSP metrics could indicate phenology change in the LSP curve, even if in reality it is indicating a change in the ratio of vegetation/ non-vegetation in the monitored area [119]. Wrong assumptions about the homogeneity of a region can also be made. For example, a forest can still have heterogeneous LSP due to species distribution and microclimatic conditions [115]. As a result, even homogeneous plots of the same species can reveal phenology variability caused by differences in site conditions or ecotope.

Moreover, the timing of green-up that is extracted from satellite time-series is often more related to understory canopy than to overstory [120]. For instance, during early and in-between growing stages in a tropical dry forest the understory vegetation develops its leaves as a response to the first rains in the beginning of the growing season [31]. These misinterpretations can be circumvented by visually inspecting vegetation structures and categories in the study area with the use of very high resolution images (e.g. Google Earth images) or *in situ* data [106]. Nevertheless, alternative approaches have proposed to scale-up species-specific field-based measurements to the landscape scale with the introduction of the Landscape Phenology Index, allowing for comparability with 250 m to 1 km LSP products [121]. This index utilizes the phenocluster concept, by aggregating community phenologies (individual phenologies of the same species that cover a representative population phenology area), and is an area-weighted average of all community phenologies over the area of study [121].

4.4 Temporal Scale Issues

Most of the disagreement between ground phenology and LSP is connected to the lower temporal resolution of the remote sensing product. Large data gaps in a time series could result in lower accuracy during interpolation. Particularly, when canopy growth or senescence is rapid, low temporal resolution products cannot accurately detect the transition dates [31]. Additionally, when field-observed phenological stages correspond to very subtle differences, these might not be detectable in satellite-measured LSP due to spectral and temporal deficiencies of satellite data. For instance, as pointed out in the study of Misra et al. [48], bud break is measured in ground phenology, but is reported as undetectable in LSP because this phenomenon is spatially too small to sufficiently influence the signal in the NIR band of a satellite sensor. In addition, bud burst signals intermixed with pre-existing understory could also contribute to the poor detection of early phenophases [48]. This is why LSP mainly focuses on phenophases that can be detected and allow for scaling up. Since ground phenology and land surface phenology have different definitions, it is almost impossible to get perfect temporal alignment in terms of specific day of the year. However, the general patterns at the start of the season as observed by field and satellite measurements are assumed to have a moderate relation, because they both look at the starting points in the cycle of vegetation development [48]. Nevertheless, one must acknowledge that in these type of comparisons, one is trying to compare a spatial integral with observations of individual plants of single species or even only traits thereof.

5 Recent LSP Advances, Tools and Products

5.1 New Trends and Advances

Cloud computing (CC) and machine learning allow for faster processing in LSP retrieval. This is especially advantageous when dealing with big data of satellite imagery, which demand for high-performance processes that are not available from a single computer. CC transfers the image processing from a scientist's personal computer to an online server. Time series from all available satellite image scenes can be easily generated through CC. For instance, the Google Earth Engine (GEE) server has been used to retrieve LSP over the North Hemisphere from VEGETATION and PROBA-V time series [122]. Other studies that estimated LSP through GEE include those of Li et al. [123], Venkatappa et al. [124], and Workie and Debella [125]. Freely accessible cloud computing platforms apart from GEE include Amazon Web Services (AWS) Open Data, TerraScope Virtual Machine, and the 'PhenologyMetrics' algorithm (see Sect. 5.2).

In addition, data cube technologies have become popular for processing remote sensing data. Image data cubes are "large collections of temporal, multivariate datasets typically consisting of analysis ready multispectral Earth observation data" [126]. The

Committee of Earth Observation Satellites (CEOS) created Open Data Cube to accommodate this concept. Data cubes can be used for LSP estimation. Li et al. [127] used this technology to study changes in vegetation green-up dates. Data cubes allow for the inclusion of all available imagery over very large extents. This can generate temporally detailed and geographically expansive LSP estimations.

Similarly, machine-learning techniques allow for the incorporation of very large data inputs. There is potential for machine learning to be used with data cubes and multi-source earth observation data. Until now, machine learning has been applied to predict ground-based phenophases or LSP from daily pheno-tower data. In detail, it has been used to learn and detect phenological patterns in numerous ground digital images [128, 129], and to fill spatiotemporal ground-based phenology to help forecast LSP with remote sensing and meteorological data [130]. The last study showed moderate-to-high potential for LSP estimation with RS through machine learning. The advantages of machine learning for LSP estimation were included in the DATimeS software (developed in 2019), with twelve machine learning fitting algorithms for time series analysis of phenology data (see Sect. 5.2). Machine learning techniques that enhance LSP are just starting to gain more ground.

Lastly, as seen previously, one of the long-standing difficulties in LSP estimation was, until recently, the accurate determination of EOS phenology metrics. One solution is to take an ensemble approach, such as taking the average of two methods. Yuan et al. [132] applied this technique by averaging the result of the midpoint and double logistical fitting to determine EOS. Moreover, it was recently discovered that for an accurate estimation of autumn phenology one needs to combine sensors and satellite data. Lu et al. [133] found that autumn phenology derived from fluorescence satellite data had higher correspondence with gross primary production (GPP) autumn phenology than autumn phenology derived from vegetation indices. Wang et al. [134] found similar results, where the EOS was estimated earlier with fluorescence satellite data data, followed by NDVI and vegetation optical depth estimations. This means that photosynthetic activity decreases before any changes in leaf color can be detected, and that the decrease in vegetation water content is the last stage of senescence. These results were consistent globally and shed light on the underlying structural and functional processes of autumn senescence.

5.2 Open-Source LSP Software

There are a number of open-source LSP estimation software. TIMESAT is a software package that enables the extraction of seasonality parameters. Its most recent version includes "Seasonal and Trend decomposition using Loess" (Version 3.3, 2017) [135], and plans the incorporation of Landsat and Sentinel-2 data [9]. PhenoSat produces LSP information from vegetation index time series. It has seven different smoothing algorithms, it recognizes more than one growth season in each year, and can focus on periods within a season [136, 137]. Verbesselt et al. [138] developed the "Breaks For Additive Seasonal Trend" method to extract seasonal and trend elements from time series to detect vegetation greenness. Examples include its use to determine grassland trends and phenology of the Flint Hills ecoregion [139], or to examine seasonal trends of vegetation on military training grounds [140]. Further, Frantz et al. [91] created the "Spline analysis of Time Series" algorithm to derive LSP by fitting spline models to remotely sensed time series. Twenty metrics per pixel are generated and relate to specific dates, and the length and amplitude of seasons. The Joint Research Centre provides "Software for the Processing and Interpretation of Remotely Sensed Image Time Series", through which LSP SOS and EOS are calculated from 10-day composite images for both single and double growing seasons with the threshold technique [142–146]. Forkel et al. [146, 147] created functions to analyse seasonal trends and trend changes in Earth Observation time series with the 'greenbrown' package in R [148]. Also, the 'phenex' package in R has functions for analysis of LSP data [149]. Lastly, the Ecopotential Virtual Library packaged the 'phenex' algorithm in an online workflow ("Estimation of phenology metrics – PhenologyMetrics") created by the Centre for Research and Technology Hellas [150]. It can derive three LSP metrics from NDVI time series during vegetation growth. The advantages include the estimation of multiple vegetation cycles in a growing period [151] and online processing without the need for high processing capabilities.

5.3 Global LSP Products

Some of the global LSP products are the MODIS Land Cover Dynamics product (MCD12Q2), the VIIRS Global Land Surface Phenology (GLSP) product, and the Vegetation Index and Phenology (VIP) Phenology (VIPPHEN) global product, which produce yearly LSP metrics (see Table 4).

Table 4. Global LSP products: MODIS Land Cover Dynamics product (MCD12Q2), VIIRS Global Land Surface Phenology product (GLSP), Making Earth System Data Records for Use in Research Environments (MEaSUREs) Vegetation Index and Phenology (VIP) global dataset. Information retrieved from Gray et al. [152], USGS [153], and X. Zhang, Liu, et al. [42]. Source [38].

Global LSP products	Timespan	Source	Spatial Resolution
MCD12Q2	2001 to end 2017	EVI2 from MODIS BRDF Adjusted Reflectance (NBAR)	500 m
VIIRS GLSP	2012 to Present	EVI2 from daily VIIRS BRDF NBAR	500 m
MEaSUREs VIP	1981 to end 2014	NDVI and EVI2 from AVHRR N07, N09, N11, N14 datasets from 1981–1999; MODIS Terra MOD09 Surface Reflectance from 2000–2014	5600 m
HLS	2013 to Present	Surface Reflectance and Top of Atmophere brightness data from Landsat 8 and Sentinel-2A and Sentinel-2B	30 m

The MCD12Q2 product is an LSP product that provides global LSP metrics derived from satellite image time series. If values are missing in an area due to cloud cover or other causes, the gaps are filled with good quality values from the year before or the following [152]. This product can be used in areas with two growing seasons [34]. The VIIRS LSP product can also estimate phenology for various vegetation types and climate systems [42]. The MEaSUREs VIP product is defined with a moving average window of three years in order to eliminate noise, and is accompanied with a reliability value to help determine data quality [153]. Lastly, the HLS surface reflectance dataset [154] currently has global coverage and can be used to derive LSP time series with observations available every 2 to 3 days [103].

6   Conclusions

This review pointed out that the use of multi-source Earth observation data, such as the HLS product, can reduce limitations that are connected to the spatial and temporal resolution of LSP. Medium spatial resolution LSP products will be more accurate at a temporal resolution of less than 16 days. Moreover, the EOS is harder to estimate from remote sensing data because canopy greenness diminishes gradually during autumn, making the transitions not very apparent. However, combined use of optical, microwave, and fluorescence RS could provide better insight to this phenomenon.

This review also showed that validation efforts should ideally include sites at least equal to the pixel size of the sensor in order to reduce the observers' subjectivity and the uncertainties of the measurements. However, the sensor's pixel size can cover a large area on the ground, making frequent site visits particularly unfeasible. Drone-mounted cameras could potentially provide a solution to this issue. Generally, studies should use phenology towers or mounted digital cameras to reduce the validation workload; mainly, because traditional field work for the collection of phenology data is often very hard to conduct for small science teams. In addition, researchers should be aware of the plant species composition in a mixed pixel, to better understand the VI response.

Lastly, Earth observation time series of higher spatial and temporal resolution bring a multitude of opportunities. Monitoring vegetation at individual stands could become possible. Large amounts of Earth observation data ask for high-performance processing methods; however cloud solutions for data storage and processing as well as machine learning workflows are freely accessible, facilitating big data processing. Moreover, data cubes allow for a new viewpoint on data analysis. This makes the previous technologies suitable for LSP estimation. Overall, the recent progress and future prospects of LSP estimation with multispectral remote sensing reviewed in this article will be able to support several of the United Nations Sustainable Development Goals and the Aichi Biodiversity Targets through developing Essential Biodiversity Variables that correspond to the Group on Earth Observation initiatives.

Acknowledgements. The authors acknowledge valuable suggestions and support from Giorgos Kordelas and George Kazakis. This review study has been partially funded and supported by the European Union's Horizon 2020 Coordination and Support Action under Grant Agreement No. 952111, EOTiST (https://cordis.europa.eu/project/id/952111).

References

1. Lieth, H.: Purposes of a phenology book. In: Lieth, H. (ed.) Phenology and Seasonality Modeling. Ecological Studies, vol. 8, pp. 3–19. Springer, Heidelberg (1974). https://doi.org/10.1007/978-3-642-51863-8_1

2. USA-NPN: Phenology Networks around the World. https://www.usanpn.org/partner/gapon (2020). Accessed 14 Jan 2020

3. Karkauskaite, P., Tagesson, T., Fensholt, R.: Evaluation of the plant phenology index (PPI), NDVI and EVI for start-of-season trend analysis of the Northern Hemisphere boreal zone. Remote Sens. 9, 1–21 (2017). https://doi.org/10.3390/rs9050485

4. Rosemartin, A.H., Crimmins, T.M., Enquist, C.A.F., et al.: Organizing phenological data resources to inform natural resource conservation. Biol. Conserv. 173, 90–97 (2014). https://doi.org/10.1016/j.biocon.2013.07.003

5. Munson, S.M., Long, A.L.: Climate drives shifts in grass reproductive phenology across the western USA. New Phytol. 213, 1945–1955 (2017). https://doi.org/10.1111/nph.14327

6. Arfin Khan, M.A.S., Beierkuhnlein, C., Kreyling, J., et al.: Phenological sensitivity of early and late flowering species under seasonal warming and altered precipitation in a seminatural temperate Grassland ecosystem. Ecosystems 21, 1306–1320 (2018). https://doi.org/10.1007/s10021-017-0220-2

7. Zhao, J., Wang, Y., Zhang, Z., et al.: The variations of land surface phenology in Northeast China and its responses to climate change from 1982 to 2013. Remote Sens. 8, 1–23 (2016). https://doi.org/10.3390/rs8050400

8. Sousa, D., Small, C., Spalton, A., Kwarteng, A.: Coupled spatiotemporal characterization of monsoon cloud cover and vegetation phenology. Remote Sens. 11, 1–22 (2019). https://doi.org/10.3390/rs11101203

9. Kuenzer, C., Dech, S, Wagner, W.: Remote Sensing Time Series. Remote Sensing and Digital Image Processing, pp 225–245 (2015). https://doi.org/10.1007/978-3-319-15967-6

10. Bradley, B.A., Jacob, R.W., Hermance, J.F., Mustard, J.F.: A curve fitting procedure to derive inter-annual phenologies from time series of noisy satellite NDVI data. Remote Sens. Environ. 106, 137–145 (2007). https://doi.org/10.1016/j.rse.2006.08.002

11. García-Feced, C., Weissteiner, C.J., Baraldi, A., et al.: Semi-natural vegetation in agricultural land: European map and links to ecosystem service supply. Agron. Sustain. Dev. 35, 273–283 (2014). https://doi.org/10.1007/s13593-014-0238-1

12. de Beurs, K.M., Henebry, G.M.: Land surface phenology, climatic variation, and institutional change: analyzing agricultural land cover change in Kazakhstan. Remote Sens. Environ. 89, 497–509 (2004). https://doi.org/10.1016/j.rse.2003.11.006

13. de Beurs, K.M., Henebry, G.M.: Land surface phenology and temperature variation in the International Geosphere-Biosphere Program high-latitude transects. Glob. Change Biol. 11, 779–790 (2005). https://doi.org/10.1111/j.1365-2486.2005.00949.x

14. Elmore, A.J., Stylinski, C.D., Pradhan, K.: Synergistic use of citizen science and remote sensing for continental-scale measurements of forest tree phenology. Remote Sens. 8, 1–16 (2016). https://doi.org/10.3390/rs8060502

15. Wang, Y., Zhao, J., Zhou, Y., Zhang, H.: Variation and trends of landscape dynamics, land surface phenology and net primary production of the Appalachian Mountains. J. Appl. Remote Sens. 6, 061708 (2012). https://doi.org/10.1117/1.jrs.6.061708

16. Chuvieco, E.: Fundamentals of Satellite Remote Sensing: An Environmental Approach, 2nd edn. Taylor & Francis (2016)

17. USA-NPN: USA National Phenology Network (2019). http://dx.doi.org/10.5066/F7X D0ZRK. Accessed 17 Sept 2019

18. NEON: NEON Science-About (2019). https://www.neonscience.org/about. Accessed 6 Nov 2019

19. PEP725: About the Pan European Phenology Project PEP725 (2019). http://www.pep725. eu/index.php. Accessed 26 Sept 2019

20. GLOBE: Overview - GLOBE (2019). https://www.globe.gov/about/overview. Accessed 26 Sept 2019

21. Salas, E.A.L.: Waveform LiDAR concepts and applications for potential vegetation phenology monitoring and modeling: a comprehensive review. Geo-Spatial Inf. Sci. **00**, 1–22 (2020). https://doi.org/10.1080/10095020.2020.1761763

22. Mascolo, L., Lopez-Sanchez, J.M., Vicente-Guijalba, F., et al.: A complete procedure for crop phenology estimation with PolSAR data based on the complex Wishart Classifier. IEEE Trans. Geosci. Remote Sens. **54**, 6505–6515 (2016). https://doi.org/10.1109/TGRS. 2016.2585744

23. Cota, N., Kasetkasem, T., Rakwatin, P., et al.: Rice phenology estimation using SAR time-series data. In: 2015 6th International Conference of Information and Communication Technology for Embedded Systems (IC-ICTES), pp. 1–5 (2015)

24. Alemu, W.G., Henebry, G.M., Melesse, A.M.: Land surface phenologies and seasonalities in the US prairie pothole region coupling AMSR passive microwave data with the USDA cropland data layer. Remote Sens. **11** (2019). https://doi.org/10.3390/rs11212550

25. Dannenberg, M., Wang, X., Yan, D., Smith, W.: Phenological characteristics of global ecosystems based on optical, fluorescence, and microwave remote sensing. Remote Sens. **12** (2020).https://doi.org/10.3390/rs12040671

26. Joiner, J., Yoshida, Y., Vasilkov, A.P., et al.: The seasonal cycle of satellite chlorophyll fluorescence observations and its relationship to vegetation phenology and ecosystem atmosphere carbon exchange. Remote Sens. Environ. **152**, 375–391 (2014). https://doi.org/10. 1016/j.rse.2014.06.022

27. Skakun, P.S., Ju, J., Claverie, M., et al.: Harmonized Landsat Sentinel-2 (HLS) Product User ' s Guide (2018)

28. Li, Z., Zhang, H.K., Roy, D.P., et al.: Landsat 15-m Panchromatic-Assisted Downscaling (LPAD) of the 30-m reflective wavelength bands to Sentinel-2 20-m resolution. Remote Sens. **9**, 1–18 (2017). https://doi.org/10.3390/rs9070755

29. Pouliot, D., Latifovic, R., Pasher, J., Duffe, J.: Landsat super-resolution enhancement using convolution neural networks and Sentinel-2 for training. Remote Sens. **10**, 1–18 (2018). https://doi.org/10.3390/rs10030394

30. Beck, P.S.A., Jönsson, P., Høgda, K.A., et al.: A ground-validated NDVI dataset for monitoring vegetation dynamics and mapping phenology in Fennoscandia and the Kola peninsula. Int. J. Remote Sens. **28**, 4311–4330 (2007). https://doi.org/10.1080/01431160701241936

31. Rankine, C., Sánchez-Azofeifa, G.A., Guzmán, J.A., et al.: Comparing MODIS and near-surface vegetation indexes for monitoring tropical dry forest phenology along a successional gradient using optical phenology towers. Environ. Res. Lett. **12**, 105007 (2017). https://doi. org/10.1088/1748-9326/aa838c

32. de Beurs, K.M., Henebry, G.M.: Chapter 9, Spatio-Temporal Statistical Methods for Modelling Land Surface Phenology. In: Phenological Research: Methods for Environmental and Climate Change Analysis. pp. 177–208 (2010)

33. Zeng, L., Wardlow, B.D., Xiang, D., et al.: A review of vegetation phenological metrics extraction using time-series, multispectral satellite data. Remote Sens. Environ. **237**, 111511 (2020). https://doi.org/10.1016/j.rse.2019.111511

34. Henebry, G.M., de Beurs, K.M.: Chapter 21-Remote sensing of land surface phenology: a prospectus. In: Phenology: An Integrative Environmental Science, pp 483–502 (2013)

35. Reed, B.C., Schwartz, M.D., Xiao, X.: Remote sensing phenology. In: Noormets, A. (ed.) Phenology of Ecosystem Processes, pp 231–246. Springer, New York (2009). https://doi. org/10.1007/978-1-4419-0026-5_10

36. Morisette, J.T., Richardson, A.D., Knapp, A.K., et al.: Tracking the rhythm of the seasons in the face of global change: phenological research in the 21st century. Front Ecol. Environ. **7**, 253–260 (2009). https://doi.org/10.1890/070217

37. Helman, D.: Land surface phenology: what do we really 'see' from space? Sci. Total Environ. **618**, 665–673 (2018). https://doi.org/10.1016/j.scitotenv.2017.07.237

38. Soubry, I., Manakos, I., Kalaitzidis, C.: Recent advances in land surface phenology estimation with multispectral sensing. In: Proceeding of the 7th International Conference on Geographical Information Systems, Theory, Applications and Management (GISTAM 2021). SCITEPRESS -Science and Technology Publications, Lda, pp. 134–145 (2021)

39. Khare, S., Drolet, G., Sylvain, J.D., et al.: Assessment of spatio-temporal patterns of black spruce bud phenology across Quebec based on MODIS-NDVI time series and field observations. Remote Sens. **11**, 1–16 (2019). https://doi.org/10.3390/rs11232745

40. Cui, T., Martz, L., Lamb, E.G., et al.: Comparison of grassland phenology derived from MODIS satellite and PhenoCam near-surface remote sensing in north America. Can. J. Remote Sens. **45**, 1–16 (2019). https://doi.org/10.1080/07038992.2019.1674643

41. Moon, M., Zhang, X., Henebry, G.M., et al.: Long-term continuity in land surface phenology measurements: a comparative assessment of the MODIS land cover dynamics and VIIRS land surface phenology products. Remote Sens. Environ. **226**, 74–92 (2019). https://doi.org/ 10.1016/j.rse.2019.03.034

42. Zhang, X., Liu, L., Liu, Y., et al.: Generation and evaluation of the VIIRS land surface phenology product. Remote Sens. Environ. **216**, 212–229 (2018). https://doi.org/10.1016/j. rse.2018.06.047

43. Fischer, A.: A model for the seasonal variations of vegetation indices in coarse resolution data and its inversion to extract crop parameters. Remote Sens. Environ. **48**, 220–230 (1994). https://doi.org/10.1016/0034-4257(94)90143-0

44. Wunderle, S., Neuhaus, C.: AVHRR Master Data Set Handbook - Deliverable 16 (WP 7). Bern (2020)

45. Zhang, X., Friedl, M.A., Schaaf, C.B., et al.: Monitoring vegetation phenology using MODIS. Remote Sens. Environ. **84**, 471–475 (2003). https://doi.org/10.1016/S0034-425 7(02)00135-9

46. Wu, C., Peng, D., Soudani, K., et al.: Land surface phenology derived from normalized difference vegetation index (NDVI) at global FLUXNET sites. Agric. Meteorol. **233**, 171–182 (2017). https://doi.org/10.1016/j.agrformet.2016.11.193

47. Cai, Z., Jönsson, P., Jin, H., Eklundh, L.: Performance of smoothing methods for reconstructing NDVI time-series and estimating vegetation phenology from MODIS data. Remote Sens. **9**, 20–22 (2017). https://doi.org/10.3390/rs9121271

48. Misra, G., Buras, A., Menzel, A.: Effects of different methods on the comparison between land surface and ground phenology - A methodological case study from South-Western Germany. Remote Sens. **8**, 1–18 (2016). https://doi.org/10.3390/rs8090753

49. Cui, T., Martz, L., Zhao, L., Guo, X.: Investigating the impact of the temporal resolution of MODIS data on measured phenology in the prairie grasslands. GIScience Remote Sens. **57**, 395–410 (2020). https://doi.org/10.1080/15481603.2020.1723279

50. ESA: Terra/Aqua MODIS. Earth Online (2020). https://earth.esa.int/web/guest/missions/ 3rd-party-missions/current-missions/terraaqua-modis. Accessed 8 Nov 2020

51. Zhang, X., Jayavelu, S., Liu, L., et al.: Evaluation of land surface phenology from VIIRS data using time series of PhenoCam imagery. Agric. Meteorol. **137–149**,(2018). https://doi. org/10.1016/j.agrformet.2018.03.003

52. Zhang, X., Liu, L., Yan, D.: Comparisons of global land surface seasonality and phenology derived from AVHRR, MODIS, and VIIRS data. J. Geophys. Res. Biogeosciences **122**, 1506–1525 (2017). https://doi.org/10.1002/2017JG003811
53. NASA EARTHDATA (2020) Visible Infrared Imaging Radiometer Suite (VIIRS). https://earthdata.nasa.gov/earth-observation-data/near-real-time/download-nrt-data/viirs-nrt#ed-corrected-reflectance. Accessed 8 Nov 2020
54. Sobrino, J.A., Julien, Y., Soria, G.: Phenology estimation from meteosat second generation data. IEEE J. Sel. Top. Appl. Earth Obs. Remote Sens. **6**, 1653–1659 (2013). https://doi.org/10.1109/JSTARS.2013.2259577
55. Yan, D., Zhang, X., Yu, Y., Guo, W.: Characterizing land cover impacts on the responses of land surface phenology to the rainy season in the Congo basin. Remote Sens. **9** (2017). https://doi.org/10.3390/rs9050461
56. Schmid, J.: The SEVIRI instrument (2000)
57. Miura, T., Nagai, S., Takeuchi, M., et al.: Improved Characterisation of vegetation and land surface seasonal dynamics in central Japan with Himawari-8 hypertemporal data. Sci. Rep. **9**, 1–12 (2019). https://doi.org/10.1038/s41598-019-52076-x
58. Ma, X., Huete, A., Tran, N.N., et al.: Sun-angle effects on remote-sensing phenology observed and modelled using Himawari-8. Remote Sens. **12**,(2020). https://doi.org/10.3390/RS12081339
59. Yan, D., Zhang, X., Nagai, S., et al.: Evaluating land surface phenology from the advanced Himawari Imager using observations from MODIS and the Phenological Eyes Network. Int. J. Appl. Earth Obs. Geoinf. **79**, 71–83 (2019). https://doi.org/10.1016/j.jag.2019.02.011
60. eoPortal Directory: Himawari-8 and 9 (2020). https://directory.eoportal.org/web/eoportal/satellite-missions/h/himawari-8-9. Accessed 8 Nov 2020
61. Fisher, J.I., Mustard, J.F., Vadeboncoeur, M.A.: Green leaf phenology at Landsat resolution: scaling from the field to the satellite. Remote Sens. Environ. **100**, 265–279 (2006). https://doi.org/10.1016/j.rse.2005.10.022
62. Melaas, E.K., Friedl, M.A., Zhu, Z.: Detecting interannual variation in deciduous broadleaf forest phenology using Landsat TM/ETM+ data. Remote Sens. Environ. **132**, 176–185 (2013). https://doi.org/10.1016/j.rse.2013.01.011
63. Liu, J., Heiskanen, J., Aynekulu, E., et al.: Land cover characterization in West Sudanian savannas using seasonal features from annual landsat time series. Remote Sens. **8**, 1–18 (2016). https://doi.org/10.3390/rs8050365
64. Dethier, B.E., Ashley, M.D., Blair, B., Hopp, R.J.: Phenology satellite experiment. In: Symposium on Significant Results Obtained from the Earth Resources Technology Satellite. Goddard Space Flight Center, New Carrollton, Maryland, pp. 157–165 (1973)
65. eoPortal Directory: Landsat-1 to 8. https://directory.eoportal.org/web/eoportal/satellite-missions/l/landsat-1-3 (2020). Accessed 8 Nov 2020
66. Solano-Correa, Y.T., Bovolo, F., Bruzzone, L., Fernández-Prieto, D.: Automatic derivation of cropland phenological parameters by adaptive non-parametric regression of Sentinel-2 NDVI time series. Int. Geosci. Remote Sens. Symp. 1946–1949 (2018). https://doi.org/10.1109/IGARSS.2018.8519264
67. Vrieling, A., Meroni, M., Darvishzadeh, R., et al.: Vegetation phenology from Sentinel-2 and field cameras for a Dutch barrier island. Remote Sens. Environ. **215**, 517–529 (2018). https://doi.org/10.1016/j.rse.2018.03.014
68. Cai, Z.: Vegetation Observation in the Big Data Era : Sentinel-2 data for mapping the seasonality of land vegetation. Lund University, Faculty of Science (2019)
69. Löw, M., Koukal, T.: Phenology Modelling and Forest Disturbance Mapping with Sentinel-2 time series in Austria (2020)
70. ESA: Sentinel-2 MSI Introduction (2020). https://sentinel.esa.int/web/sentinel/user-guides/sentinel-2-msi. Accessed 8 Nov 2020

71. Cheng, Y., Vrieling, A., Fava, F., et al.: Phenology of short vegetation cycles in a Kenyan rangeland from PlanetScope and Sentinel-2. Remote Sens. Environ. **248**, 112004 (2020). https://doi.org/10.1016/j.rse.2020.112004

72. Myers, E., Kerekes, J., Daughtry, C., Russ, A.: Assessing the impact of satellite revisit rate on estimation of corn phenological transition timing through shape model fitting. Remote Sens. **11**, 1–21 (2019). https://doi.org/10.3390/rs11212558

73. Sadeh, Y., Zhu, X., Chenu, K., Dunkerley, D.: Sowing date detection at the field scale using CubeSats remote sensing. Comput. Electron. Agric. **157**, 568–580 (2019). https://doi.org/10.1016/j.compag.2019.01.042

74. Chen, B., Jin, Y., Brown, P.: An enhanced bloom index for quantifying floral phenology using multi-scale remote sensing observations. ISPRS J. Photogramm. Remote Sens. **156**, 108–120 (2019). https://doi.org/10.1016/j.isprsjprs.2019.08.006

75. Planet: Planet Imagery-Product Specifications. Plant Labs Inc 2018 (2018). https://www.planet.com/products/planet-imagery/. Accessed 9 Sept 2020

76. ESA: Planet. eoPortal Dir (2020). https://directory.eoportal.org/web/eoportal/satellite-missions/p/planet. Accessed 9 Sept 2020

77. ESA: PlanetScope (2020). https://earth.esa.int/web/guest/missions/3rd-party-missions/current-missions/planetscope. Accessed 18 May 2020

78. Gao, F., Anderson, M., Daughtry, C., et al.: A within-season approach for detecting early growth stages in corn and soybean using high temporal and spatial resolution imagery. Remote Sens. Environ. **242**, 111752 (2020). https://doi.org/10.1016/j.rse.2020.111752

79. Herrmann, I., Bdolach, E., Montekyo, Y., et al.: Assessment of maize yield and phenology by drone-mounted superspectral camera. Precis. Agric. **21**, 51–76 (2020). https://doi.org/10.1007/s11119-019-09659-5

80. Manivasagam, V.S., Kaplan, G., Rozenstein, O.: Developing transformation functions for VENμS and Sentinel-2 surface reflectance over Israel. Remote Sens. **11** (2019). https://doi.org/10.3390/rs11141710

81. ESA: VENμS - Vegetation an Environment monitoring on a New MicroSatellite. Obs. Earth Environ. Surv. Mission Sensors (2020). https://directory.eoportal.org/web/eoportal/satellite-missions/v-w-x-y-z/venus. Accessed 8 Mar 2020

82. Wulder, M.A., Loveland, T.R., Roy, D.P., et al.: Current status of Landsat program, science, and applications. Remote Sens. Environ. **225**, 127–147 (2019). https://doi.org/10.1016/j.rse.2019.02.015

83. Storey, J., Roy, D.P., Masek, J., et al.: A note on the temporary misregistration of Landsat-8 Operational Land Imager (OLI) and Sentinel-2 Multi Spectral Instrument (MSI) imagery. Remote Sens. Environ. **186**, 121–122 (2016). https://doi.org/10.1016/j.rse.2016.08.025

84. Li, J., Roy, D.P.: A global analysis of Sentinel-2a, Sentinel-2b and Landsat-8 data revisit intervals and implications for terrestrial monitoring. Remote Sens 9 (2017). https://doi.org/10.3390/rs9090902

85. ESA: VENμS (Vegetation and Environment monitoring on a New MicroSatellite). eoPortal Dir (2020). https://directory.eoportal.org/web/eoportal/satellite-missions/v-w-x-y-z/venus. Accessed 8 Sept 2020

86. Trenkle, T., Driggers, P.: Joint polar satellite system. Sensors, System Next-Generation Satellite XV (2019). https://www.jpss.noaa.gov/mission_and_instruments.html. Accessed 18 Sept 2019

87. eoPortal Directory: Satellite Missions Database (2020). https://eoportal.org/web/eoportal/satellite-missions. Accessed 3 Dec 2020

88. UrtheCast: UrtheDaily. https://www.urthecast.com/missions/urthedaily/ (2020). Accessed 9 Sept 2020

89. Fraser, A.D., Massom, R.A., Michael, K.J.: A method for compositing MODIS satellite images to remove cloud cover. Int. Geosci. Remote Sens. Symp. **3**, 639–641 (2009). https://doi.org/10.1109/IGARSS.2009.5417841

90. Zhu, X., Chen, J., Gao, F., et al.: An enhanced spatial and temporal adaptive reflectance fusion model for complex heterogeneous regions. Remote Sens. Environ. **114**, 2610–2623 (2010). https://doi.org/10.1016/j.rse.2010.05.032

91. Frantz, D., Stellmes, M., Röder, A., et al.: Improving the spatial resolution of land surface phenology by fusing medium- and coarse-resolution inputs. IEEE Trans. Geosci. Remote Sens. **54**, 4153–4164 (2016). https://doi.org/10.1109/TGRS.2016.2537929

92. Frantz, D.: FORCE-Landsat + Sentinel-2 analysis ready data and beyond. Remote Sens. **11**, 1–21 (2019). https://doi.org/10.3390/rs11091124

93. Stellmes, M., Frantz, D., Röder, A., Waske, B.: Multi-annual Phenology Metrics at Landsat Scale in Data-Sparse Areas Fusing annual medium resolution phenology data with ImproPhe. In: 3rd EARSeL SIG LU/LC and NASA LCLUC joint Workshop, Chania (2018)

94. Melaas, E.K., Sulla-Menashe, D., Gray, J.M., et al.: Multisite analysis of land surface phenology in North American temperate and boreal deciduous forests from Landsat. Remote Sens. Environ. **186**, 452–464 (2016). https://doi.org/10.1016/j.rse.2016.09.014

95. Skakun, S., Roger, J.C., Vermote, E.F., et al.: Automatic sub-pixel co-registration of Landsat-8 Operational Land Imager and Sentinel-2A Multi-Spectral Instrument images using phase correlation and machine learning based mapping. Int. J. Digit. Earth **10**, 1253–1269 (2017). https://doi.org/10.1080/17538947.2017.1304586

96. Claverie, M., Ju, J., Masek, J.G., et al.: The Harmonized Landsat and Sentinel-2 surface reflectance data set. Remote Sens. Environ. **219**, 145–161 (2018). https://doi.org/10.1016/j.rse.2018.09.002

97. Claverie, M., Masek, J.G.: Harmonized Landsat-8 Sentinel-2 (HLS) Product User's Guide (2017)

98. Nijland, W., Bolton, D.K., Coops, N.C., Stenhouse, G.: Imaging phenology; scaling from camera plots to landscapes. Remote Sens. Environ. **177**, 13–20 (2016). https://doi.org/10.1016/j.rse.2016.02.018

99. Jönsson, P., Cai, Z., Melaas, E., et al.: A method for robust estimation of vegetation seasonality from Landsat and Sentinel-2 time series data. Remote Sens. **10**, 1–13 (2018). https://doi.org/10.3390/rs10040635

100. Kowalski, K., Senf, C., Hostert, P., Pflugmacher, D.: Characterizing spring phenology of temperate broadleaf forests using Landsat and Sentinel-2 time series. Int. J. Appl. Earth Obs. Geoinf. **92**, 1–8 (2020). https://doi.org/10.1016/j.jag.2020.102172

101. Li, S., Ganguly, S., Dungan, J.L., et al.: Sentinel-2 MSI radiometric characterization and cross-calibration with Landsat-8 OLI. Adv. Remote Sens. **06**, 147–159 (2017). https://doi.org/10.4236/ars.2017.62011

102. Chrysafis, I., Mallinis, G., Siachalou, S., Patias, P.: Assessing the relationships between growing stock volume and Sentinel-2 imagery in a mediterranean forest ecosystem. Remote Sens. Lett. **8**, 508–517 (2017). https://doi.org/10.1080/2150704X.2017.1295479

103. Masek, J., Ju, J., Roger, J., et al.: HLS Operational Land Imager Surface Reflectance and TOA Brightness Daily Global 30 m v2.0. In: NASA EOSDIS L. Process. DAAC (2021). https://lpdaac.usgs.gov/news/release-of-harmonized-landsat-and-sentinel-2-hls-version-20/. Accessed 27 Jan 2022

104. Friedl, M., Bolton, D., Moon, M., et al.: MuSLI Multi-Source Land Surface Phenology (MS-LSP) Product User Guide (2020)

105. Eklundh, L., Jin, H., Schubert, P., et al.: An optical sensor network for vegetation phenology monitoring and satellite data calibration. Sensors **11**, 7678–7709 (2011). https://doi.org/10.3390/s110807678

106. Soto-Berelov, M., Jones, S., Farmer, E., et al.: Chapter 2: Review of validation standards of Earth Observation derived biophysical products. In: AusCover Good Practice Guidelines: A technical handbook supporting calibration and validation activities of remotely sensed data products. Pp. 8–30 (2015)
107. Gerstmann, H., Doktor, D., Gläßer, C., Möller, M.: PHASE: a geostatistical model for the Kriging-based spatial prediction of crop phenology using public phenological and climatological observations. Comput. Electron. Agric. **127**, 726–738 (2016). https://doi.org/10.1016/j.compag.2016.07.032
108. Hess, M., Barralis, G., Bleiholder, H., et al.: Use of the extended BBCH scale - General for the descriptions of the growth stages of mono- and dicotyledonous weed species. Weed Res. **37**, 433–441 (1997). https://doi.org/10.1046/j.1365-3180.1997.d01-70.x
109. Meier, U.: Growth stages of mono-and dicotyledonous plants-BBCH Monograph (2001)
110. Fischer, A.: A simple model for the temporal variations of NDVI at regional scale over agricultural countries. Validation with ground radiometric measurements. Int. J. Remote Sens. **15**, 1421–1446 (1994). https://doi.org/10.1080/01431169408954175
111. Nasahara, K.N., Nagai, S.: Review: development of an in situ observation network for terrestrial ecological remote sensing: the Phenological Eyes Network (PEN). Ecol. Res. **30**, 211–223 (2015). https://doi.org/10.1007/s11284-014-1239-x
112. PEN: Phenological Eyes Network (PEN) (2020). http://www.pheno-eye.org/. Accessed 11 May 2020
113. Templ, B., Koch, E., Bolmgren, K., et al.: Pan European Phenological database (PEP725): a single point of access for European data. Int. J. Biometeorol. **62**, 1109–1113 (2018). https://doi.org/10.1007/s00484-018-1512-8
114. PHENOCAM: About the PhenoCam Data (2020). http://phenocam.us/. Accessed 12 Nov 2020
115. Zhang, X., Wang, J., Gao, F., et al.: Exploration of scaling effects on coarse resolution land surface phenology. Remote Sens. Environ. **190**, 318–330 (2017). https://doi.org/10.1016/j.rse.2017.01.001
116. Tang, J., Körner, C., Muraoka, H., et al.: Emerging opportunities and challenges in phenology: a review. Ecosphere **7**, 1–17 (2016). https://doi.org/10.1002/ecs2.1436
117. Elmendorf, S.C., Jones, K.D., Cook, B.I., et al.: The plant phenology monitoring design for the national ecological observatory network. Ecosphere **7**, 1–16 (2016). https://doi.org/10.1002/ecs2.1303
118. Tan, B., Gao, F., Tan, B., et al.: An enhanced TIMESAT algorithm for estimating vegetation phenology metrics from MODIS Data. IEEE J. Sel. Top. Appl. Earth Obs. Remote Sens. **4**, 361–371 (2011). https://doi.org/10.1109/JSTARS.2010.2075916
119. Helman, D., Lensky, I.M., Tessler, N., Osem, Y.: A phenology-based method for monitoring woody and herbaceous vegetation in mediterranean forests from NDVI time series. Remote Sens. **7**, 12314–12335 (2015). https://doi.org/10.3390/rs70912314
120. Ryu, Y., Lee, G., Jeon, S., et al.: Monitoring multi-layer canopy spring phenology of temperate deciduous and evergreen forests using low-cost spectral sensors. Remote Sens. Environ. **149**, 227–238 (2014). https://doi.org/10.1016/j.rse.2014.04.015
121. Liang, L., Schwartz, M.D.: Landscape phenology: an integrative approach to seasonal vegetation dynamics. Landsc. Ecol. **24**, 465–472 (2009). https://doi.org/10.1007/s10980-009-9328-x
122. Bórnez, K., Richardson, A.D., Verger, A., et al.: Evaluation of VEGETATION and PROBA-V phenology using phenocam and eddy covariance data. Remote Sens. **12** (2020). https://doi.org/10.3390/RS12183077
123. Li, G., Jiang, C., Cheng, T., Bai, J.: Grazing alters the phenology of alpine steppe by changing the surface physical environment on the northeast Qinghai-Tibet Plateau. China J. Environ. Manage. **248**, 109257 (2019). https://doi.org/10.1016/j.jenvman.2019.07.028

124. Venkatappa, M., Sasaki, N., Shrestha, R.P., et al.: Determination of vegetation thresholds for assessing land use and land use changes in Cambodia using the Google Earth Engine cloud-computing platform. Remote Sens. **11**, 1–30 (2019). https://doi.org/10.3390/rs1113 1514

125. Workie, T.G., Debella, H.J.: Climate change and its effects on vegetation phenology across ecoregions of Ethiopia. Glob. Ecol. Conserv. **13**, 1–13 (2018). https://doi.org/10.1016/j. gecco.2017.e00366

126. Kopp, S., Becker, P., Doshi, A., et al.: Achieving the full vision of earth observation data cubes. Data **4** (2019). https://doi.org/10.3390/data4030094

127. Li, J., Feng, X., Yin, J., Chen, F.: Change analysis of spring vegetation green-up date in Qinba Mountains under the support of spatiotemporal data cube. J. Sens. **2020**, 1–12 (2020). https://doi.org/10.1155/2020/6413654

128. Almeida, J., Dos Santos, J.A., Alberton, B., et al.: Applying machine learning based on multiscale classifiers to detect remote phenology patterns in Cerrado savanna trees. Ecol. Inform. **23**, 49–61 (2014). https://doi.org/10.1016/j.ecoinf.2013.06.011

129. Ryu, D., Kim, T.K., Won, M.S., et al.: Developing a machine learning based automatic plant phenology observation system. In: AGU Fall Meeting Abstracts. AA(Interdisciplinary Program in Agricultural and Forest Meteorology, Seoul National University, Seoul, South Korea), AB(Seoul National University, Seoul, Korea, Republic of (South)), AC(Forest Ecology and Climate Change Division, National Institute of For, pp. B51H-2020 (2018)

130. Czernecki, B., Nowosad, J., Jabłońska, K.: Machine learning modeling of plant phenology based on coupling satellite and gridded meteorological dataset. Int. J. Biometeorol. **62**, 1297–1309 (2018). https://doi.org/10.1007/s00484-018-1534-2

131. Yuan, H., Wu, C., Lu, L., Wang, X.: A new algorithm predicting the end of growth at five evergreen conifer forests based on nighttime temperature and the enhanced vegetation index. ISPRS J. Photogramm. Remote Sens. **144**, 390–399 (2018). https://doi.org/10.1016/j.isprsj prs.2018.08.013

132. Yuan, H., Wu, C., Gu, C., Wang, X.: Evidence for satellite observed changes in the relative influence of climate indicators on autumn phenology over the Northern Hemisphere. Glob. Planet Change **187**, 103131 (2020). https://doi.org/10.1016/j.gloplacha.2020.103131

133. Lu, X., Liu, Z., Zhou, Y., et al.: Comparison of phenology estimated from reflectance-based indices and solar-induced chlorophyll fluorescence (SIF) observations in a temperate forest using GPP-based phenology as the standard. Remote Sens. **10** (2018). https://doi.org/10. 3390/rs10060932

134. Wang, X., Dannenberg, M.P., Yan, D., et al.: Globally consistent patterns of asynchrony in vegetation phenology derived from optical, microwave, and fluorescence satellite data. J. Geophys. Res. Biogeosciences **125**, 1–15 (2020). https://doi.org/10.1029/2020JG005732

135. Eklundh, L.: Welcome to the TIMESAT pages! TIMESAT (2017). http://www.nateko.lu.se/ TIMESAT/timesat.asp. Accessed 25 Sep 2019

136. Rodrigues, A., Marcal, A.R.S., Cunha, M.: Monitoring vegetation dynamics inferred by satellite data using the PhenoSat tool. IEEE Trans. Geosci. Remote Sens. **51**, 2096–2104 (2013). https://doi.org/10.1109/TGRS.2012.2223475

137. Marcal, A.R.S., Cunha, M.: PhenoSat (2020). https://www.fc.up.pt/PhenoSat/software.html. Accessed 3 Mar 2020

138. Verbesselt, J., Hyndman, R., Newnham, G., Culvenor, D.: Detecting trend and seasonal changes in satellite image time series. Remote Sens. Environ. **114**, 106–115 (2010). https:// doi.org/10.1016/j.rse.2009.08.014

139. Masters, P., Gehrt, J., Keast, R., et al.: Statistical Analysis of Grassland Trends and Phenology using Satellite Time Series Imagery of the Flint Hills Ecoregion. Manhattan (2016)

140. Hutchinson, J.M.S., Jacquin, A., Hutchinson, S.L., Verbesselt, J.: Monitoring vegetation change and dynamics on U.S. army training lands using satellite image time series analysis. J. Environ. Manage. **150**, 355–366 (2015). https://doi.org/10.1016/j.jenvman.2014.08.002

141. Rembold, F., Tote, C., Eerens, H., et al.: SPIRITS. Addis Ababa, Ethiopia (2013)

142. Rembold, F., Meroni, M., Urbano, F., et al.: Remote sensing time series analysis for crop monitoring with the SPIRITS software: new functionalities and use examples. Front. Environ. Sci. **3**, 1–11 (2015). https://doi.org/10.3389/fenvs.2015.00046

143. Eerens, H., Haesen, D., Rembold, F., et al.: Image time series processing for agriculture monitoring. Environ. Model Softw. **53**, 154–162 (2014). https://doi.org/10.1016/j.envsoft.2013.10.021

144. Eerens, H., Dominique, H.: Software for the Processing and Interpretation of Remotely sensed Image Time Series USER'S MANUAL Version : 1.1.1 (2013)

145. Bornez, K., Verger, A., Filella, I., Penuelas, J.: Land surface phenology from Copernicus Global Land time series. In: 2017 9th International Workshop on the Analysis of Multitemporal Remote Sensing Images, MultiTemp 2017, vol. 1, pp. 17–20 (2017). https://doi.org/10.1109/Multi-Temp.2017.8035262

146. Forkel, M., Carvalhais, N., Verbesselt, J., et al.: Trend change detection in NDVI time series: effects of inter-annual variability and methodology. Remote Sens. **5**, 2113–2144 (2013). https://doi.org/10.3390/rs5052113

147. Forkel, M., Migliavacca, M., Thonicke, K., et al.: Codominant water control on global interannual variability and trends in land surface phenology and greenness. Glob. Change Biol. **21**, 3414–3435 (2015). https://doi.org/10.1111/gcb.12950

148. Forkel, M., Wutzler, T.: Greebrown - land surface phenology and trend analysis. A package for the R software. Version 2.2 (2015). http://greenbrown.r-forge.r-project.org/

149. Lange, M., Doktor, D.: Package 'phenex' (2017)

150. Nativi, S., Mazzetti, P., Santoro, M.: Deliverable No : D10.1 Design of the ECOPOTENTIAL Virtual Laboratory, Version V1.0 (Final Draft) (2016)

151. Guigoz, Y.: Estimation of phenology metrics (PhenologyMetrics) - ECOPotential Virtual Laboratory - ESSI Lab Documentation (2017). https://confluence.geodab.eu/pages/viewpage.action?pageId=2458817. Accessed 25 Sept 2019

152. Gray, J., Sulla-Menasche, D., Friedl, M.: Lp Daac - Mcd12Q2 (2019). https://lpdaac.usgs.gov/products/mcd12q2v006/. Accessed 26 Sept 2019

153. USGS: VIPPHEN_NDVI v004 (2019). https://lpdaac.usgs.gov/products/vipphen_ndvi v004/. Accessed 7 Jan 2020

154. Bolton, D., Gray, J.M., Melaas, E.K., et al.: Continental-scale land surface phenology from harmonized Landsat 8 and Sentinel-2 imagery. Remote Sens. Environ. **240**, 1–16 (2020). https://doi.org/10.1016/j.rse.2020.111685

Analytical Hierarchical Processing to Delineate Artificial Groundwater Recharge Zones

Rami Al-Ruzouq[1](✉) ⓘ, Abdallah Shanableh[1] ⓘ, Abdullah Gokhan Yilmaz[2] ⓘ,
Sunanda Mukherjee[1] ⓘ, and Mohamad Ali Khalil[1] ⓘ

[1] Civil and Environmental Engineering Department, University of Sharjah, Sharjah 27272, UAE
ralruzouq@sharjah.ac.ae
[2] Department of Engineering, La Trobe University, Melbourne VIC 3086, Australia

Abstract. Scarcity of water has impacted the Gulf countries and one of them is the United Arab Emirates (UAE). Among the many possibilities, a viable approach for water preservation in arid regions is Artificial Groundwater Recharging (AGR). Fresh water from multiple sources are fetched and reserved in aquifers and pumped out during lean phases. This research endeavors to delineate AGR zones in Northern part of UAE taking into account of precipitation, drainage density, geomorphology, geology, groundwater level, total dissolved solids, elevation, lineament density, and distance from residences with the aid of Remote Sensing (RS) and Geographic Information System (GIS). Parameters were measured to criteria weightings by Analytical Hierarchical Process (AHP), and then overlay analysis was performed to deduce the potential AGR map. The map was categorized in a scale ranging from very high suitability to low suitability. More than 20% of the total area was highly suitable for AGR. Geology and geomorphology were identified to be the significant factors for determination of the potential zones.

Keywords: Artificial groundwater recharge · Geographic information system · Remote sensing · United Arab Emirates · Analytical hierarchical process

1 Introduction

Urban sprawls and densely populated cities have created an immense urge on higher water consumption to fulfill several needs. The primary hurdle faced by any developing nation is inadvertent urbanization, deficient water resources and unproductive management of water supply and distribution. Developing nations specifically in arid and semi-arid climatic regions are still gathering reforms and resources to combat such issues [1]. Countries closer to sea or ocean focus on desalination and reservoir storage as water preservation practices. Since the 1990s, another technique that has gained attention is artificial groundwater recharge (AGR)[2]. It has paved the way for arid and semi-arid nations as one of the most sustainable approaches to water conservation due to higher evaporation rates [3].

The United Arab Emirates (UAE) is one of the most brisk developing nations. Its population leaped sharply from 531,265 in 1975 to 10 million in 2022 [4]. The niche

© The Author(s), under exclusive license to Springer Nature Switzerland AG 2023
C. Grueau et al. (Eds.): GISTAM 2021/2022, CCIS 1908, pp. 38–51, 2023.
https://doi.org/10.1007/978-3-031-44112-7_3

lifestyle of the UAE population demands water consumption of about 550 L per capita per day in 2020 compared to the global average of 170–300 L per capita per day which is 82% higher than any countries [5]. Note that the UAE is located in an arid climate region with limited freshwater resources and scarce rainfall [6]. Approximately, 51% of the UAE's water supply comes from freshwater resources [7]. Thus the UAE depends on alternative water preservation practices such as desalination, water storage units, artificial groundwater recharge to meet demands during lean periods. As the country's temperature rises approximately 50 degrees Celsius in summers, any surface water storage takes a heavy toll on the economy due to high evaporation rates. Therefore the country is indulging into more sustainable practices of water conservation by adopting AGR. AGR is a scientific water storage technique of available water into aquifers and use it in dry periods for agriculture, industrial and potable purposes [8]. Many studies [8–14] have been implemented through Remote Sensing (RS) and Geographic Information System (GIS) for AGR demarcation and implementation. Primary step is to identify potential zones where RS & GIS comes to a rescue. Humble decision making approach is adapted for AGR demarcation and then tools of machine learning like artificial neural network, support vector machine, random forest and so on are further integrated to validate the data if we analyse previous researches for AGR across the globe [10, 11, 14–18]. Less AGR studies have been carried out in UAE and specially central northern UAE covering Emirates of Sharjah, Umm al Quwain, Ras al Khaimah, Fujairah and Ajman [19]. Therefore this research made an attempt to demarcate potential AGR sites for the previously mentioned emirates.

The research utilized multicriteria decision analysis by Saaty 1990 paired with weighted overlay analysis to identify potential zones for AGR. The study was carried out at the Central northern Emirates including emirates of Sharjah, Fujairah, ras al Khaimah, Umm al Quwain, Ajman, and portions of Oman. This study utlized more previous studies for analysing ranking and weighting of Analytical Hierarchical Process (AHP) compared to previous research [19] and also calculated the percentage of the area suitable and not suitable for AGR. Nine thematic layers were prepared: precipitation, drainage stream density (DSD), geomorphology, geology, groundwater level, Total Dissolved Solids (TDS), elevation, lineament density (LD), distance from residential areas. The research aims to delineate suitable locations for implementing AGR by employing RS, GIS, AHP, and the weighted overlay technique. The main objectives of this study is summarized within the following:

- Investigating suitable zones for AGR in Sharjah by utilizing RS and GIS.
- Identifying and mapping spatial thematic layers for AGR zonation: precipitation, drainage stream density (DSD), geomorphology, geology, groundwater level, Total Dissolved Solids (TDS), elevation, lineament density (LD), Euclidean distance from residential areas.
- Employing AHP and weighted overlay techniques to obtain AGR map.
- Calculating percentage of area suitable for AGR and the primary factors governing it.

2 Study Area

The United Arab Emirates is a Mediterranean country located in the western part of Asia and is surrounded by the Arabian Gulf in the west and north, Gulf of Oman in the northeast, Oman in the east, and Saudi Arabia in the south (Fig. 1) [6, 20–22]. The country's water demands are met by 43% of its available groundwater resources. However, due to its arid climatic condition, the country has reserves of only 640 billion cubic meters (BCM) of groundwater, and 20 BCM is fresh [21, 23]. The country receives approximately 102 mm of mean annual rainfall within cities and 130 mm in mountains with temperatures rising to 48 degrees during summer months in desert [21, 23, 24]. Majority of the land is covered with sand and so forth, the sand dune aquifer system dominates the geographic region. Other classifications of the aquifer system are northern limestone, ophiolite, eastern gravel, western gravel, and coastal marshes [25]. Five major cities of northern UAE have been covered in this study which includes Sharjah, Umm al Quwain, Ras al Khaimah, Ajman, and Fujairah. This region comprises equal proportions of all the aquifers classes.

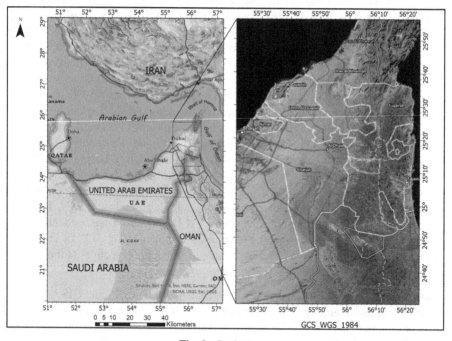

Fig. 1. Study Area.

3 Methodology and Data Processing

Figure 2 demonstrates the methodology developed for identifying potential zones for AGR. Suitable remote sensing imageries such as digital elevation model (DEM), Landsat 8, enhanced thematic mapper plus, historical data of precipitation, and salinity were used to prepare desired thematic layers contributing to AGR potential zones. The previously discussed factors pprecipitation, DSD, geomorphology, geology, groundwater level, TDS, elevation, lineament density, euclidean distance from residential areas were developed as spatial thematic layers in ArcGIS Pro. Five classes ranging from 1 to 9 derived from Natural Breaks technique, have been assigned to each layer, with 1 representing least suitability and 9 as most suitable. AHP technique helped to identify weights of each criteria. To obtain the final potential map, weighted overlay analysis was performed.

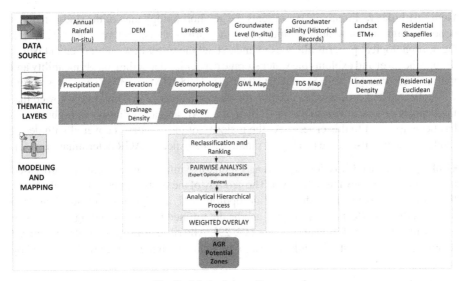

Fig. 2. Methodology Framework.

3.1 Thematic Layers Preparation

This section demonstrates the data collection, image processing aspects and its correlation to the potentiality of AGR, of each parameter primarily considered for the objective of the study. Delineating suitable AGR zones were achieved through nine spatial parameters: Precipitation, DSD, geomorphology, geology, groundwater level, TDS, elevation, lineament density, euclidean distance from residential areas [26–28]. The detailed discussion about the layers are mentioned in the following paragraphs.

Precipitation. National Centre for Meteorology, UAE, was referred to deduce annual total rainfall historical data from 2003–2017 refer, Fig. 3(a). Data was collected from the rain gauge stations and coordinates of each station were utilized to develop the point map. Inverse distance weighting interpolation technique further obtained the spatial layer of precipitation. The data helped to understand that the least average of annual total rainfall was recorded as 75mm for the study and ranged maximum up to 103mm. From multiple research articles it is profound that the regions receiving more rainfall is directly proportional to AGR potential zones [21, 23, 24].

Drainage Stream Density. DSD of the study area ranged from 0 to .58 per km^2 Fig. 3(b). The parameter is defined as the capacity of the total water drained through stream channels within a watershed represented as the ratio of total stream length of all orders by the total area of the drainage basin. Permeability of water decreases if DSD is higher [17, 26]. It is one of the fundamental parameters for AGR demarcation. SRTM (Shuttle Radar Topography Mission) DEM spatial data were used to develop the thematic layer [23]. Increased regional DSD can be noticed in the eastern part of the Sharjah Emirate, north and northeastern part of Ras-al-Khaimah and Umm-al-Quwain, respectively [21, 23].

Geomorphology. Figure 3(c) represents the geomorphology map of the study area: fan deposits, high and low dunes, mountain, sand, urban areas, and vegetation [21, 23]. Geomorphological patterns allow us to understand the water flow and movement below the ground level and explains the water storage capacities depending on permeability and porous landforms [17, 29]. Spatial data from Landsat8 ETM+ of 30 m spatial resolution was collected and processed to develop the thematic layer [23]. This study showed that fan deposits are most favorable for AGR in the UAE and accordingly the highest rank has been assigned to this criteria. As the majority of the country is covered with desert sand, high dunes also come in a higher ranking with respect to AGR determination, refer.

Geology. Landsat 8 was downloaded and shortwave infrared band were geo-processed to develop the geology thematic layer. The geology of the study area comprises: alluvium, limestone, gabbro, metamorphic, sand and ophiolite [21, 23]. Sand covers more than 45% of the study area. Recharging volume can be determined by understanding the porosity and assigning spaces for water holding [17, 29]. Alluvium holds more water compared to other classes. This study marked the alluvium class with the highest rank followed by sand.

Total Dissolved Solids. Historical data from **the** Ministry of Environment and Water, UAE (2015) were considered to prepare the spatial thematic layer of TDS. TDS has a great impact on the quality as it exceeds the turbidity of water which eventually determines the fit and unfit for potable use. Permeability of water with high TDS can clog pores stopping the flow through the aquifer and risks of pathogen activities increases leading to many diseases to humankind. Regions with lower values of TDS are considered to be fit for AGR zonation [30, 31]. Generally, TDS values are enormously high near to the coastal shorelines. TDS map of this study conductively portrayed that regions closer to Gulf of Oman have values of 38000 mg/l whereas the west of the study area which is covered by Arabian Gulf have TDS values of 50000 mg/l. This demonstrates the outcome that Arabian Gulf is more saline compared to Gulf of Oman.

Groundwater Level. In-situ data from bore-wells were collected within the study area and combined together making interoperability in the GIS platform to deduce the thematic layer, refer Fig. 3(d). Inverse distance weighted interpolation technique was used in ArcGIS Pro to develop the layer. The units are meters above sea level (masl). This factor helps in analyzing the hydraulic gradient of the region which eventually depends on pore pressure and atmospheric pressure at the surface level [17, 27, 32]. Higher levels of groundwater is less likely suitable for AGR [17, 32]. The thematic layers shows that the southeast Sharjah and west of Ras al-Khaimah have higher values of groundwater levels. One of the primary explanation behind this is that the region is in close proximity to the foothills and receives more rainfall which up levels the groundwater. The IDW equation is as follows [13, 21, 33]:

$$Z_0 = \frac{\sum_{i=1}^{N} z_i x d_i^{-n}}{\sum_{i=1}^{N} d_i^{-n}} \tag{1}$$

Where Z = calculated value of Z at o;

z_i = observed value at sample point I; d_i is the distance between sample point i and o; N is the number of sample points used to estimate the value at o; n is a distance decay parameter [34, 35].

Elevation. SRTM DEM of 30m spatial resolution were downloaded and used for developing the thematic layer. The elevation is as low as zero meters above sea level (masl) near shore lines and as high as 1112 masl in the mountains for the study area, Fig. 3(e). Elevation is inversely proportional to AGR zonation which demonstrates that inferior elevation values are more appropriate for AGR [9, 27, 35–37]. It analyses the accumulation capacity of water and its flow direction through the aquifers. Few regions within Fujairah and Ras-al Khaimah have elevation above 1000 masl.

Lineament Density. Linear features such as fractures and folds were extracted from satellite images and then spatial maps were processed. It has direct proportionality to AGR suitability. Availability of groundwater and potential available aquifers can be determined from his parameter. It also determines the secondary porosity. Higher values of LD can be witnessed in Fujairah. Generally, from previous research it has been concluded that a zone of around 300m closer to any folds and fractures of the earth composition can be considered suitable for AGR [29].

Distance from Residences. To develop this layer, shapefiles of residential areas were mapped and then Euclidean distance was calculated to prepare the thematic layer, refer Fig. 3(f). For sustainable AGR sites the distance from residences factor needs to be considered. AGR needs to be designed at optimum distance from the densely located city considering water pumping factors to required places as well as closer proximity to pipelines [8, 35]. Higher the distance from residences more suitability for AGR.

3.2 Analytical Hierarchical Process

AHP is a structured multi-criteria decision making (MCDM) procedure. It utilizes experts' opinions to determine the weights and rank of each parameter. AHP has been used by researchers in various groundwater studies and site selection studies [8, 21, 23, 33, 38–41]. This study employs AHP for selecting potential zones for the AGR. An important step in AHP is prioritizing the parameters and assigning them weights, as discussed below.

Weighting the Parameters. The influencing factors were arranged as a structured hierarchy and the pairwise comparison matrix were formed to confirm the consistency of the weights. The weights of the all 9 selected parameters were placed in a square matrix

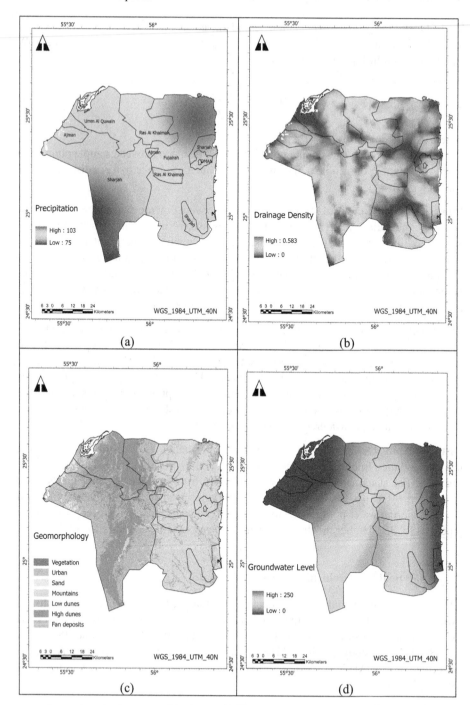

Fig. 3. Thematic Layers [19].

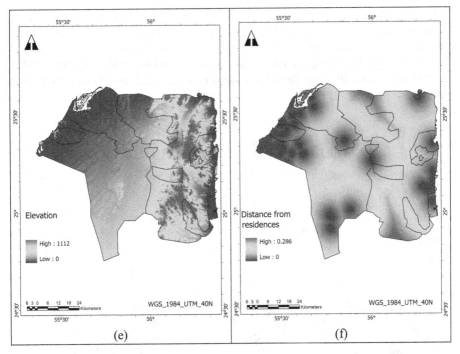

Fig. 3. (*continued*)

keeping all the diagonal values as 1. The diagonal of the pairwise matrix was kept 1 when both the parameters have equal importance over the other. The relative importance of the parameters were analyzed using the principal eigenvalue along with the normalized right eigenvector of the matrix [21, 23, 42, 43]. On a scale of 1–9 of relative importance by Saaty [44] all the parameters were ranked. Highest rank 9 was assigned to criteria with highest influence on the decision. Measurements of consistency were done by checking the randomized and consistency index as well as the consistency ratio.

Consistency Ratio. CR allows the glance for the subjectivity of determined weights through a pairwise matrix. In order to confirm the consistency of the pairwise comparison matrix, consistency index (CI), consistency ratio (CR) and randomized index (RI) were obtained. CR is defined as the degree of consistency of the comparison matrix prepared with respect to parameters and its weights. The value of CR must be less than 0.01 for the consistency of the matrix to be maintained [21, 23, 43]. The CR can be derived using the following equations [44]:

$$CI = \frac{\lambda max - n}{n - 1} \tag{2}$$

$$RI = \frac{1.98 \times (n - 1)}{n} \tag{3}$$

$$CR = \frac{CI}{RI} \tag{4}$$

CI is a consistency index, RI is a randomized index (average of CI values of the comparison matrix), CR is a consistency ratio, λ_{max} is the maximum eigenvalue of a comparison matrix and n is the order of the comparison matrix. The calculated CR equals.007 < .01, which supports the weighting model and the AHP technique [21, 45]. Fig. 4 Demonstrates the weights of the utilized thematic layer associated with AGR in percentage.

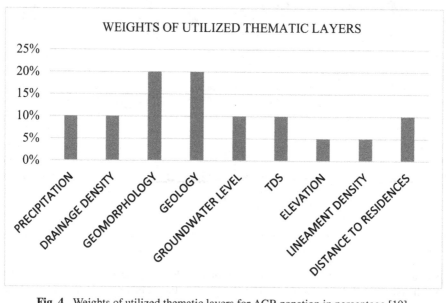

Fig. 4. Weights of utilized thematic layers for AGR zonation in percentage [19].

4   Results and Discussion

The potential AGR was estimated and mapped using AHP approach, refer Fig. 5. The map was categorized on the basis of ordinal scale into 6 classes: "very high", "high", "moderate high", "moderate low", "low", and "very low".

Following points were concluded from the AGR map:

(i) The very high zone is located in the central part of Ras al Khaimah. The properties of the input parameters have geology- alluvium, geomorphology -fan deposits, precipitation of 91 mm, groundwater level 102 masl, drainage density at .38 per km^2, TDS 1862 mg/l, distance from residences .14 m, elevation of 87 m and lineament density of .05 per km^2.

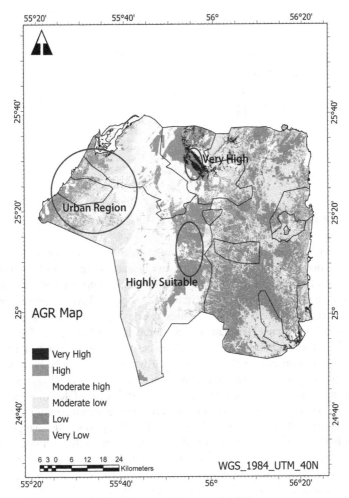

Fig. 5. Potential zones of AGR.

(ii) The "high" zone is located in the north-eastern and central-eastern part of Sharjah. This region also comprises geomorphology- fan deposits, geology-alluvium. This region is near the foothills of the Al-hajjar Mountains and thus comprises many suitable qualities of geology and geomorphological characteristics for AGR. TDS of 1300 mg/l were noted in this region.

(iii) Table 1 demonstrates the area in percentage for each class of AGR.

Table 1. Percentage of area for AGR classes.

AGR Classes	Percentage of Area
Very High	1%
High	21%
Moderate - High	30%
Moderate - Low	34%
Low	12%
Very Low	1%

5 Conclusion

The main objective of this paper was to determine locations which are suitable for AGR, delineate them using AHP and be able to get an estimate of the proportion of study area which can benefit from AGR techniques. To go about this approach, 9 main parameters were found to be governing AGR site suitability. A weighted AHP process was utilized to rank these parameters and then a weighted overlay analysis was done to obtain the final AGR suitability map. The map was clustered in 6 areas ranging from very high suitability to very low suitability. Several inferences were then drawn from the resulting map. The north-central part of Ras Al Khaimah was observed to be lying in the most highly suitable zone while another major portion of Ras Al Khaimah and Sharjah were seen to be lying in the zone characterized as high suitability for AGR. Another reason was the high elevation and mountainous region which received high amounts of precipitation and this in turn caused high amounts of fan and alluvial deposits in these regions. On the other hand, both the shorelines were found not suitable for AGR due to the presence of high salinity. Similarly, dense populations in the urban locations of the eastern parts also made these areas unsuitable for AGR. Out of the total study area, 20% was estimated to be a highly suitable category, 30% as moderate-high, and 12% as low. This was done using ArcGIS Pro and utilizing pixel sizes as the deciding factor. Semi-arid and arid countries such as those in the gulf can highly benefit from this research methodology to demarcate and locate potential locations and zones suitable for AGR techniques. As the world moves into a stage where water becomes more and more a scarcity, the methodology described in this paper can serve as a guiding tool at the least to help find suitable locations for AGR and reduce the stress caused by water scarcity.

References

1. Dawoud, M.A.: The development of integrated water resource information management system in arid regions. Arab. J. Geosci. **6**, 1601–1612 (2013). https://doi.org/10.1007/s12517-011-0449-6
2. Bhunia, G.S.: An approach to demarcate groundwater recharge potential zone using geospatial technology. Appl. Water Sci. **10**(6), 1–12 (2020). https://doi.org/10.1007/s13201-020-01231-1

3. Al-Othman, A.A.: Enhancing groundwater recharge in arid region- a case study from central Saudi Arabia. Sci. Res. Essays **6**, 2757–2762 (2011). https://doi.org/10.5897/SRE11.173
4. United Arab Emirates Population Statistics 2022—GMI. https://www.globalmediainsight.com/blog/uae-population-statistics/. Accessed 24 Jan 2022
5. How much water does the UAE use per day? – SidmartinBio. https://www.sidmartinbio.org/how-much-water-does-the-uae-use-per-day/. Accessed 24 Jan 2022
6. Shanableh, A., Al-Ruzouq, R., Yilmaz, A.G., et al.: Effects of land cover change on urban floods and rainwater harvesting: a case study in Sharjah, UAE. Water (Switzerland) 10 (2018). https://doi.org/10.3390/w10050631
7. Country Commercial Guides: United Arab Emirates - Water. Int. Trade Adm. (2020). https://next.trade.gov/country-commercial-guides/united-arab-emirates-water. Accessed 24 Jan 2022
8. Riad, P.H.S., Billib, M., Hassan, A.A., et al.: Application of the overlay weighted model and boolean logic to determine the best locations for artificial recharge of groundwater. J. Urban Environ. Eng. **5**, 57–66 (2011). https://doi.org/10.4090/juee.2011.v5n2.057066
9. Rahimi, S., Shadman, M., Ali Abbaspour, R.: Using combined AHP-genetic algorithm in artificial groundwater recharge site selection of Gareh Bygone Plain. Iran. Environ. Earth Sci. **72**, 1979–1992 (2014). https://doi.org/10.1007/s12665-014-3109-9
10. Ghayoumian, J., Saravi, M.M.: Application of GIS techniques to determine areas most suitable for artificial groundwater recharge in a coastal aquifer in southern Iran. **30**, 364–374 (2007). https://doi.org/10.1016/j.jseaes.2006.11.002
11. Samadder, R.K., Kumar, S., Gupta, R.P.: Paleochannels and their potential for artificial groundwater recharge in the western Ganga plains. J. Hydrol. **400**, 154–164 (2011). https://doi.org/10.1016/j.jhydrol.2011.01.039
12. Dinesh Kumar, M., Patel, A., Ravindranath, R., Singh, O.P.: Chasing a mirage: water harvesting and artificial recharge in naturally water-scarce regions. Econ. Polit. Wkly. **43**, 61–71 (2008)
13. Chandramohan, R., Vignesh, N.S., Krishnamoorthy, R.: Remote sensing and GIS based approach for delineation of artificial recharge sites in Palani Taluk. Dindigul. Dist. **8**, 698–706 (2017)
14. Mokarram, M., Saber, A., Mohammadizadeh, P., Abdolali, A.: Determination of artificial recharge location using analytic hierarchy process and Dempster-Shafer theory. Environ. Earth Sci. **79**,(2020). https://doi.org/10.1007/s12665-020-08994-5
15. Bhowmick, P.: A review on GIS based Fuzzy and Boolean logic modelling approach to identify the suitable sites for Artificial Recharge. Sch. J. Eng. Technol. (SJET) **2**, 316–319 (2014)
16. Mokarram, M., Negahban, S., Abdolali, A., Ghasemi, M.M.: Using GIS-based order weight average (OWA) methods to predict suitable locations for the artificial recharge of groundwater (2021)
17. Khan, A., Govil, H., Taloor, A.K., Kumar, G.: Identification of artificial groundwater recharge sites in parts of Yamuna River basin India based on remote sensing and geographical information system. Groundw. Sustain. Dev. **11**, 100415 (2020). https://doi.org/10.1016/j.gsd.2020.100415
18. Selvarani, A.G., Maheswaran, G., Elangovan, K.: Identification of artificial recharge sites for Noyyal River basin using GIS and remote sensing. J. Ind. Soc. Remote Sens. **45**, 67–77 (2017). https://doi.org/10.1007/s12524-015-0542-5
19. Al-Ruzouq, R., Shanableh, A., Yilmaz, A., et al.: Multicriteria Spatial Analysis to Map Artificial Groundwater Recharge Zones: Northern UAE, pp. 255–262 (2021). https://doi.org/10.5220/0010432802550262
20. Murad, A.A., Nuaimi, H., Hammadi, M.: Comprehensive assessment of water resources in the United Arab Emirates (UAE). Water Resour. Manage. **21**, 1449–1463 (2007). https://doi.org/10.1007/s11269-006-9093-4

21. Al-Ruzouq, R., Shanableh, A., Yilmaz, A.G., et al.: Dam site suitability mapping and analysis using an integrated GIS and machine learning approach. Water (Switzerland) **11**,(2019). https://doi.org/10.3390/w11091880

22. Al-ruzouq, R., Shanableh, A.: Macro and micro geo-spatial environment consideration for landfill site selection in Sharjah, United Arab Emirates, pp. 1–15 (2018)

23. Al-ruzouq, R., Shanableh, A., Merabtene, T., et al.: Potential Groundwater Zone Mapping Based on Geo-Hydrological Considerations and Multi-Criteria Spatial Analysis : North UAE, pp. 1–40 (2019)

24. Sherif, M.M., Ebraheem, A.M., Al Mulla, M.M., Shetty, A.V.: New system for the assessment of annual groundwater recharge from rainfall in the United Arab Emirates. Environ. Earth Sci. **77**,(2018). https://doi.org/10.1007/s12665-018-7591-3

25. Saif, A., Matri, A.: Assessment of Artificial Groundwater Recharge in Some Wadies in UAE by using Isotope Hydrology Techniques (2008)

26. Rais, S., Javed, A.: Identification of Artificial Recharge Sites in Manchi Basin, Eastern Rajasthan (India) Using Remote Sensing and GIS Techniques, pp. 162–175 (2014)

27. Alrehaili, A.M., Hussein, M.T.: Use of remote sensing, GIS and groundwater monitoring to estimate artificial groundwater recharge in Riyadh, Saudi Arabia. Arab. J. Geosci. **5**, 1367–1377 (2012). https://doi.org/10.1007/s12517-011-0306-7

28. Chowdary, V.M.: Delineation of groundwater recharge zones and identification of artificial recharge sites in West Medinipur district, West Bengal, using RS, GIS and MCDM techniques, pp. 1209–1222 (2010). https://doi.org/10.1007/s12665-009-0110-9

29. Senanayake, I.P., Dissanayake, D.M.D.O.K., Mayadunna, B.B., Weerasekera, W.L.: Geoscience Frontiers an approach to delineate groundwater recharge potential sites in Ambalantota, Sri Lanka using GIS techniques. Geosci. Front. **7**, 115–124 (2016). https://doi.org/10.1016/j.gsf.2015.03.002

30. Nasiri, H., Boloorani, A.D., Sabokbar, H.A.F., et al.: Determining the most suitable areas for artificial groundwater recharge via an integrated PROMETHEE II-AHP method in GIS environment (case study: Garabaygan Basin, Iran). Environ. Monit. Assess. **185**, 707–718 (2013). https://doi.org/10.1007/s10661-012-2586-0

31. Kazakis, N.: Delineation of suitable zones for the application of Managed Aquifer Recharge (MAR) in coastal aquifers using quantitative parameters and the analytical hierarchy process. Water (Switzerland) **10**,(2018). https://doi.org/10.3390/w10060804

32. Hammouri, N., Al-Amoush, H., Al-Raggad, M., Harahsheh, S.: Groundwater recharge zones mapping using GIS: a case study in Southern part of Jordan Valley, Jordan. Arab. J. Geosci. **7**, 2815–2829 (2014). https://doi.org/10.1007/s12517-013-0995-1

33. Agarwal, R., Garg, P.K.: Remote sensing and GIS based groundwater potential & recharge zones mapping using multi-criteria decision making technique. Water Resour. Manage. **30**, 243–260 (2016). https://doi.org/10.1007/s11269-015-1159-8

34. Rukundo, E., Doğan, A.: Dominant influencing factors of groundwater recharge spatial patterns in Ergene river catchment, Turkey. Water (Switzerland) **11** (2019). https://doi.org/10.3390/w11040653

35. da Costa, A.M., de Salis, H.H.C., Viana, J.H.M., Pacheco, F.A.L.: Groundwater recharge potential for sustainable water use in urban areas of the Jequitiba River Basin. Brazil. Sustain. **11**,(2019). https://doi.org/10.3390/su11102955

36. Mahmoud, S.H., Alazba, A.A.: Identification of potential sites for groundwater recharge using a GIS-based decision support system in Jazan region-Saudi Arabia. Water Resour. Manage. **28**, 3319–3340 (2014). https://doi.org/10.1007/s11269-014-0681-4

37. Sharma, C.S.: Artificial groundwater recharge zones mapping using remote sensing and GIS : a case study in Indian Punjab 61–71 (2013). https://doi.org/10.1007/s00267-013-0101-1

38. Mahdavi, A., Tabatabaei, S.H., Mahdavi, R., Nouri Emamzadei, M.R.: Application of digital techniques to identify aquifer artificial recharge sites in GIS environment. Int. J. Digit. Earth **6**, 589–609 (2013). https://doi.org/10.1080/17538947.2011.638937

39. Ahmadi, M.M., Mahdavirad, H., Bakhtiari, B.: Multi-criteria analysis of site selection for groundwater recharge with treated municipal wastewater. Water Sci. Technol. **76**, 909–919 (2017). https://doi.org/10.2166/wst.2017.273

40. Rahman, M.A., Rusteberg, B., Gogu, R.C., et al.: A new spatial multi-criteria decision support tool for site selection for implementation of managed aquifer recharge. J. Environ. Manage. **99**, 61–75 (2012). https://doi.org/10.1016/j.jenvman.2012.01.003

41. Chenini, I., Ben, M.A., El, M.M.: Groundwater recharge zone mapping using GIS-based multi-criteria analysis: A case study in Central Tunisia (Maknassy Basin). Water Resour. Manage. **24**, 921–939 (2010). https://doi.org/10.1007/s11269-009-9479-1

42. Chezgi, J., Pourghasemi, H.R., Naghibi, S.A., et al.: Assessment of a spatial multi-criteria evaluation to site selection underground dams in the Alborz Province. Iran. Geocarto. Int. **31**, 628–646 (2016). https://doi.org/10.1080/10106049.2015.1073366

43. Norouzi, H., Shahmohammadi-Kalalagh, S.: Locating groundwater artificial recharge sites using random forest: a case study of Shabestar region. Iran. Environ. Earth Sci. **78**, 1–11 (2019). https://doi.org/10.1007/s12665-019-8381-2

44. Saaty, T.L.: How to make a decision: the analytic hierarchy process. Eur. J. Oper. Res. **48**, 9–26 (1990). https://doi.org/10.1016/0377-2217(90)90057-I

45. Al-Ruzouq, R., Shanableh, A., Merabtene, T., et al.: Potential groundwater zone mapping based on geo-hydrological considerations and multi-criteria spatial analysis: North UAE. CATENA **173**, 511–524 (2019). https://doi.org/10.1016/j.catena.2018.10.037

WorldView-3 Imagery and GEOBIA Method for the Urban Land Use Pattern Analysis: Case Study City of Split, Croatia

Rina Milošević[1], Silvija Šiljeg[2(✉)], and Ivan Marić[2(✉)]

[1] Hrvatsko Geografsko Društvo (HGD) Zadar, Trg Kneza Višeslava 9, 23 000 Zadar, Croatia
rmilosevi@unizd.hr
[2] Department of Geography, University of Zadar, Trg Kneza Višeslava 9, 23 000 Zadar, Croatia
{ssiljeg,imaric1}@unizd.hr

Abstract. In most urban environments, loss of natural vegetation, the reduction of open spaces, and the rapid invasive transformation of the natural environment into impervious have happened. These changes can lead to a decline in life quality and in an increase in various economic, social, ecological, and infrastructural problems and risks. The complexity of the urban environment at various scales requires the application of high spatial and temporal resolution data in the process of urban planning. The main goal of this paper was to derive specific landscape metrics characteristic for urban areas based on WV-3 very-high-resolution imagery and the GEOBIA method. A supervised machine learning technique support vector machine (SVM) was used as a classification algorithm. The derived land-cover model is evaluated using the *confusion matrix* and related accuracy metrics: *user accuracy* (UA), *producer's accuracy* (PA), *overall* accuracy (OA), and Kappa coefficient. Land-cover classification accuracy assessment resulted in moderate *overall accuracy* while aggregation of classes depending on the physical characteristics of the material increased OA. For landscape diversity and area metric analysis, aggregated classes were used in combination with user-defined polygons. In the city of Split, there is no absolute homogeneity (SHDI = 0) within any of the hexagons. Inner parts of the city have a higher SHDI than the outskirts but impervious surfaces are the dominant material. Urban planning indicators (UPIs), have been derived for statistical circles (SC) of Split settlement in Croatia. Vegetation indicators (TCR - tree cover ratio, LCR - lawn cover ratio, GCR - green cover ratio) and indicators of urbanization (SCR - street cover ratio, BCR - building cover ratio, IMR - impervious surface ratio) were derived from the derived land cover model. The UPIs values at the studied level are the reflection of the historical spatial-functional development of the Split settlement. These types of UPIs can be used at the neighborhood level of urban planning and analysis of different issues in an urban environment.

Keywords: WorldView-3 (WV3) · Shannon Diversity Index (SHDI) · Largest patch · Urban Planning Indicators (UPIs) · GEOBIA method

© The Author(s), under exclusive license to Springer Nature Switzerland AG 2023
C. Grueau et al. (Eds.): GISTAM 2021/2022, CCIS 1908, pp. 52–67, 2023.
https://doi.org/10.1007/978-3-031-44112-7_4

1 Introduction

Urbanization has led to the replacement of natural vegetation-dominated surfaces by various impervious materials. This had a significant impact on the environment. Some of the observed consequences are reduction of the open spaces [1]., increased risk of pluvial floods [2]., endangerment of the drinking water quality [3]., the appearance of the urban heat islands (UHI) [4]., various environmental pollution problems and ultimately a decline in life quality [6]. Therefore, efficient urban planning has become a central tool of governance, through which these major issues of urban development will have to be addressed [7]. This challenge requires new analytic approaches and new sources of data and information in urban planning [8].

There are numerous definitions of urban planning [9, 10]. It is regarded as a complex, technical, and political process that includes land use control, urban environment design, and environmental protection. Its primary purpose is to improve the decision-making process [11]. In the context of urban planning, there is a notion of the urban environment [12, 13]. Which is defined as a physical place that includes different land use patterns, built infrastructure, and transportation systems [14, 15]. The increasing availability of geospatial data in combination with traditional data sources could facilitate the development of new tools for understanding urban environment complexity [13]. Urban environment planning requires a multidisciplinary approach and the application of modern research methods [16, 17] through the application of various geospatial technologies (GST) [13, 18]. GST is defined as a set of methods, techniques, and procedures used in modeling of complex processes and features in different levels of detail (LoD) depending on the research purpose [19]. GST includes GIS, elements of remote sensing (RS), a global positioning system (GPS), and other related geospatial technologies [20, 21].

The application of GST enables computing of the various landscape metrics typically used to characterize and understand different types of the environment structure using the measures of the size, shape, and spatial proximity of specific land types.

In the literature, the landscape metrics mostly refer to indices developed for categorical map patterns [22]. And topographic measures [23]. Although the usage of these metrics is very broad, the most common usage is for the biodiversity [24, 25] and habitat analysis and for the evaluation of the current landscape pattern or its change through time [25]. Landscape metrics are based on the analysis of landscape pattern which is influenced by physical, social, landscape, and environment, reflecting different ecological processes and structural functions [26]. Some common metrics include landscape composition (proportion, richness, evenness, diversity) and spatial configuration (patch size and shape, connectivity, dispersed or clumped patches, neighborhood) [27].

The spatial distributions of the metrics provide new insight into landscape structure, which can be exploited in land use planning and in the construction of empirical spatial planning heuristics for sustainable urban development. Despite numerous advantages of landscape metrics, it is important to emphasize their sensitivity to image scale and extent of the study area so comparisons across time and space must be done considering the resolution [27]. Depending on the research purpose and type of the landscape there are various indicators that can be used. For the urban areas typically are used urban planning indicators (UPI) in combined with the composition and configuration. In urban pattern analysis crucial is impervious surface as an indicator of urban ecological environmental change. Accurately estimating impervious areas is essential to monitoring the urban dynamics of change and human activities and their effects on urban environmental quality [28].

UPIs serve decision-makers, with measuring performance role, in the planning of the urban environment [29]. The UPIs are usually determined at the very beginning of planning and serve as a basis for the entire planning and process design. UPIs are crucial in the monitoring of urban morphology and urban development intensity. They are derived for different purposes, among which stands out research about urban thermal islands [29, 30]. The building of sustainable cities, and sustainable urban development [31–33], and achieving sustainable urban governance [33]. The LoD and spatial resolution of data used to derive specific UPIs depend on the level (eg. local, neighborhood, metropolitan, regions) [34] or scale (macro-micro) [35] at which the urban planning process is performed. In this research, we use high-resolution WorldView-3 imagery to derive specific landscape metrics for the city of Split, Croatia. The research was performed within the INTERREG Italy- Croatia PEPSEA (Protecting the Enclosed Parts of the Sea in Adriatic from pollution) project. UPIs were calculated from a land cover model which was derived using geographic object-based image analysis (GEOBIA) [36].

2 Study Area

Split is the administrative center of Split-Dalmatia County. It is the largest city in the Dalmatia region and the second-largest city in the Republic of Croatia (HR) (Fig. 1B). At the latest census (2021), the total population of Split was 161.312. Split is located on the peninsula and surrounded by hills. Mosor hill is located on the northeast side of the city (Fig. 1C). Kozjak hill is located on the northwest side. Split is surrounded by the islands of Brač, Hvar, Šolta, and Čiovo (Fig. 1B) [54]. The city of Split consists of 92 statistical circles (SC) (Fig. 1C). A statistical circle is one of the smallest statistical spatial units in the HR. They were established in 1959 and revised in each previous census. They represent a permanent network of spatial units, covering the entire mainland of the HR [37, 54].

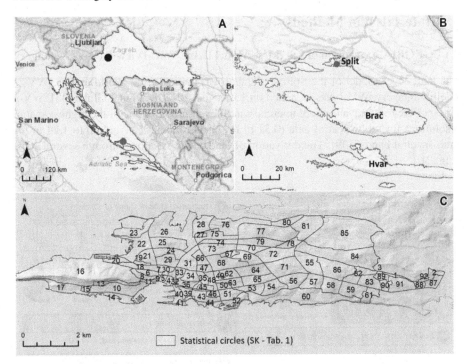

ID of the statistical circle:

1-SK0049298, 2-SK0049301, 3-SK0049310, 4-SK0109819, 5-SK0109827, 6-SK0109835, 7-SK0109843, 8-SK0109851, 9-SK0109860, 10-SK0109878, 11-SK0109886, 12-SK0109894, 13-SK0109908, 14-SK0109916, 15-SK0109924, 16-SK0109932, 17-SK0109959, 18-SK0109967, 19-SK0109975, 20-SK0109983, 21-SK0109991, 22-SK0110019, 23-SK0110027, 24-SK0110035, 25-SK0110043, 26-SK0110051, 27-SK0110060, 28-SK0110078, 29-SK0110086, 30-SK0110094, 31-SK0110108, 32-SK0110116, 33-SK0110124, 34-SK0110132, 35-SK0110159, 36-SK0110167, 37-SK0110175, 38-SK0110183, 39-SK0110191, 40-SK0110205, 41-SK0110213, 42-SK0110221, 43-SK0110230, 44-SK0110248, 45-SK0110256, 46-SK0110264, 47-SK0110272, 48-SK0110299, 49-SK0110302, 50-SK0110329, 51-SK0110337, 52-SK0110345, 53-SK0110353, 54-SK0110361, 55-SK0110370, 56-SK0110388, 57-SK0110396, 58-SK0110400, 59-SK0110418, 60-SK0110426, 61-SK0110434, 62-SK0110442, 63-SK0110469, 64-SK0110477, 65-SK0110485, 66-SK0110493, 67-SK0110507, 68-SK0110515, 69-SK0110523, 70-SK0110531, 71-SK0110540, 72-SK0110558, 73-SK0110566, 74-SK0110574, 75-SK0110582, 76-SK0110604, 77-SK0110612, 78-SK0110639, 79-SK0110647, 80-SK0110655, 81-SK0110663, 82-SK0110671, 83-SK0110680, 84-SK0110698, 85-SK0110701, 86-SK0110710, 87-SK0113034, 88-SK0113069, 89-SK0113107, 90-SK0113115, 91-SK0113123, 92-SK0148652

Fig. 1. A) Split settlement in the HR; B) location of the Split peninsula in Split-Dalmatia Country and B) statistical circles (IDs of Split settlement [54].

3 Materials and Methods

3.1 GEOBIA Extraction of Land Use Model Using WorldView-3 (WV-3) Imagery

The land cover model of the Split settlement was derived from WorldView-3 (WV-3) satellite imagery. WV-3 was launched on 13 August 2014 by Digital Globe [38]. WV-3 is one of the most advanced commercial satellites. It provides one of the highest spatial resolutions for multispectral data (0.31 m for panchromatic data and up to 1.24 m for multispectral bands) [39]. The derivation of land cover was done through several steps (Fig. 2).

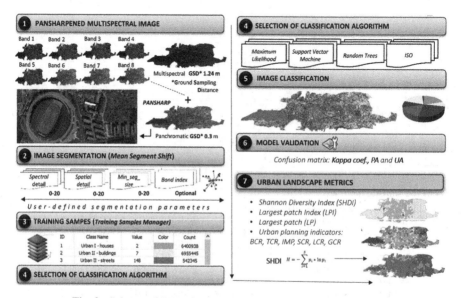

Fig. 2. Scheme of WV-3 image processing using GEOBIA method.

The first step involved the creation of a multispectral image (MS) using the *Composite bands tool*. Then spatial resolution of the MS was enhanced using a panchromatic image) [51]. This was performed in the Geomatica Banff 2018 Trial with the PANSHARP tool. The product of this process was pan-sharpened MS. The next step was the segmentation process. The Segment Mean Shift tool in ArcGIS software was used. The quality of the land cover is highly determined by the selection of user-defined parameters: *Spectral Detail, Spatial Detail, Min_Segment_Size, and Band Indexes* [54].

The Spectral Detail sets the level of importance given to the spectral differences of features in the imagery (ESRI, 2020). The Spatial Detail sets the level of importance given to the proximity between features. In both cases, values range from 1 to 20.

The *Min_Segment_Size* parameter identifies blocks of pixels that are too small (in relation to defined value) to be considered as a fragment (ESRI, 2020). All segments that are smaller than the specified value will be merged with their best-fitting neighbor segment.

Band_Indexes parameters refer to the selection of the bands used in multispectral image segmentation. It is necessary to choose bands that offer the most noticeable differences between features. However, there is no clearly defined rule about the optimal segmentation parameters values) [50]. To define the best combination for UPIs extraction, we have tested different parameter values using (Fig. 3) the visual interpretation method (*trial-and-error*)) [50].

Fig. 3. Tested segmentation parameter values [54].

Three segmented images were generated using different parameter values (Fig. 3). The visual interpretation showed that the third segmented model gave the best result (Fig. 3). In it, the values of spectral and spatial detail are high enough to separate features of similar spectral characteristics and to create not too spatially smooth classes. In this model, training samples are taken for the identification of the land cover classes. About fifty training samples were marked for each defined class ($n = 8$). In the next step, the train Esri classifier definition (.ecd) file using the Support Vector Machine (SVM) was created. Some researchers have shown that SVM in urban environments) [47] is achieving higher classification accuracy than traditional methods) [48, 54]. In the final step, the land cover model for the Split settlement was generated (Fig. 2). In future research, the accuracy assessment of land cover (overall accuracy and class by class) will be performed using the very high-resolution multispectral model generated with Mica Sense RedEdge-MX mounted on Matrix 600 Pro.

3.2 Accuracy Assessment of the Land-Cover Model

Land cover classifications derived from GIS imagery require validation against a ground truth [49]. The accuracy was determined against the digital-orthophoto (DOF) as the ground truth layer, from the portal of the State Geodetic Administration (DGU). The process of assessment was performed in ArcMap using the *confusion matrix* to summarize results from the classification method and manually interpreted land cover from the ground truth layer. To provide an assessment database, random points of specified sample size ($n = 175$) are randomly scattered across the research area using the *Create Accuracy Assessment Point tool*. The matrix was created by the *Compute Confusion matrix tool*. Accuracy was expressed with related metrics: user accuracy (UA: type error 1 or false positive), producer's accuracy (PA: type error 2 or false negative), overall accuracy (OA), and Kappa coefficient. A Python toolbox *(ZonalMetrics)* in ArcGIS was used to analyze the urban structure. The calculation of landscape metrics was performed within the user-defined zones (in this case hexagons). The first step was creating the zones using the *Create hexagons tools*. The height parameter of each hexagon was set to 200 m which resulted in the area of 54 126 m^2, Based on the user-defined parameters total Split settlement area was divided into the 546 hexagons.

Therefore, at the zonal level in this paper the next diversity and area metrics were applied:

1) **Shannon's Diversity Index (SHDI)** which represents the amount of information per patch, and it is calculated by the formula [22]:

$$SHDI = -\sum (pi * \ln pi) \, m \, i = 1$$

where is:

pi = the proportion of the statistical zone area occupied by patch type.
m = the total number of patch types.

This index, ranging in theory from 0 to infinity, estimates the average uncertainty in predicting which land cover type a randomly selected sub-unit of the landscape will belong to [53]. The minimum value of 0 means that there is no diversity within the user-defined zone.

2) **Largest Patch Index (LPI)** secludes the patch of a specific class that dominates within a predefined zone, and it is calculated by the formula [22].

$$LPI = (ni \, A) * 100 \, (6)$$

where is:

ni = area of specific LC class; A = total area of the statistical zone.

3.3 Derivation of Urban Planning Indicators (UPIs)

The UPIs for each statistical circle were derived from the generated land cover. UPIs used in this study were:

1. *Lawn Cover Ratio (LCR):* percentage of the study area that is covered by low vegetation (%);
2. *Tree Cover Ratio* (TCR): percentage of the study area that is covered by trees (%);
3. *Green Cover Ratio (GCR):* percentage of the study area that is covered by any kind of vegetation (%) (GCR = LCR + TCR);
4. *Street Cover Ratio* (SCR): percentage of the study area that is covered by concrete surfaces (%);
5. *Building Cover Ratio* (BCR): percentage of the study area that is covered by buildings (%)

Impervious Surfaces Ratio (ISR): percentage of the study area that is covered by impervious surfaces (buildings + concrete surfaces, houses) (%).

4 Results and Discussion

4.1 Land Cover Model

A total of eight land use classes have been identified and extracted; tree cover, lawn cover, street cover, buildings, houses, macadam, shadows, and other objects (Fig. 4). In addition to the functionality, the urban land use classes also differ in the type of material (physical characteristics) and can be impervious or permeable. Landscape permeability depends on an interplay between the spatial arrangement of the different land-cover types, such as houses, buildings, streets, and natural areas [40]. Based on these characteristics derived eight land-use classes were merged into three categories for which diversity and area metrics were calculated.: impervious surfaces (houses, street cover, buildings, other objects), permeable surfaces (macadam, lawn cover, tree cover), and shadows.

Shadows are observed as a deficiency in this MS imagery. This has become especially notable in the urban environment modeling where they are potentially the main source of misclassification This problem is particularly pronounced when using advanced sensors with very high resolution [41]. Therefore, in this research shadows are detected and classified as a separate category [42]. In this case study, most of them are detected on the northern side of the objects due to the Sun's position during the satellite recording and are caused by a pronounced height of specific objects. The percentage of shadow class in the total area of SK varies significantly the highest percentages (around 15%) are found in smaller statistical circles (SK0110485, SK0110361) in which tall, residential buildings predominate.

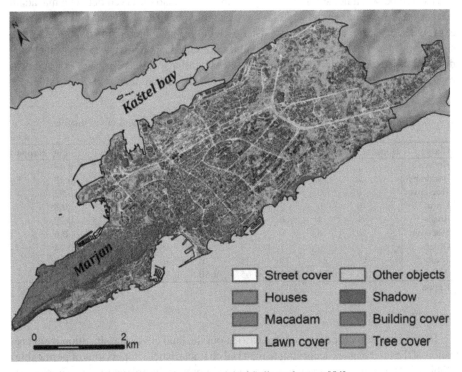

Fig. 4. Land cover model of Split settlement [54].

4.2 Land-Cover Validation

The accuracy of the eight classes of land cover was evaluated by the visual validation of points for each class (n = 25). For the overall accuracy, Landis and Kosch's Scale was used (0 -poor, 1-almost perfect) which is often used in the land-cover accuracy interpretation [43, 44]. A Kappa coefficient equal to 1 means perfect agreement whereas a value close to zero means that the agreement is no better than would be expected by chance [52]. In this study land cover is moderately accurate (0.54). The confusion matrix is presented in Tab. 1. The columns of the matrix show ground truth (referent values) and the rows show classes derived using the SVM. The diagonal shows correctly classified pixels. Misclassified pixels do not occur in the diagonal and give an indication of the confusion between the different land-cover classes in the class assignment. The highest UA is related to the tree cover (0.92) and lawn (0.8). Other objects have the lowest UA (0.24) which is expected because this class is derived by grouping the objects (transitional forms) which resulted in the highest variability in spectral characteristics within the class. Houses and buildings have the same value of UA (0.48). PA is the highest for the houses (0.8). The greatest confusion is noticed in the distinction between the buildings and roads and as well between houses and roads. Confusion was also observed between macadam surfaces that were mostly falsely classified as buildings. These misclassifications were expected because the urban areas are the most complex and challenging to model despite significant advances in GST. One of the major limitations in urban mapping is that many different urban land covers may share the same or similar spectral responses (e.g., cement roads, parking lots, cement rooftops, and other bright surface features) [45] (Table 1).

Table 1. Confusion matrix generated for eight classes of Land-cover model.

Class	Houses	Build.	Tree	Lawn	Roads	Mac.	Other	Total	UA	**Kappa**
Houses	12	2	1	2	7	0	1	25	0.48	
Buildings	2	12	1	0	9	1	0	25	0.48	
Tree cover	0	0	23	2	0	0	0	25	0.92	
Lawn	0	0	3	20	0	2	0	25	0.8	
Roads	1	4	0	0	18	2	0	25	0.72	
Macadam	0	6	0	0	1	15	3	25	0.6	
Other	0	0	1	7	1	10	6	25	0.24	
Total	15	24	29	31	36	30	10	175	0	
PA	0.80	0.50	0.79	0.65	0.50	0.50	0.60	0	0.61	
Kappa										0.54

For comparison purposes, we also carried out the land cover classification by aggregation of the land classes according to material characteristics (impervious or permeable) (Table 2). The overall accuracy is significantly improved compared to classification per functionality. However, two scenarios related to shadows were made. In the first, shadows were excluded from the accuracy assessment because they are considered a deficiency of multispectral imagery. Kappa coefficient for the classification of the impervious and permeable surfaces has increased to 0.76 and UA and PA for each class were higher than 0.8 (Table 2). Still, including the shadows in the assessment, the overall accuracy decreased to 0.67 (Table 3), but PA and UA of impervious and permeable surfaces remained high (>0.79). Detected shadows mostly (85%) obscure impermeable surfaces which results in false-negative results.

Table 2. Confusion matrix generated for aggregated classes (physical characteristics) excluding shadows.

Class	Impervious	Permeable	Total	UA	**Kappa**
Impervious	88	10	98	0.90	
Permeable	12	77	89	0.87	
Total	100	87	187	0	
PA	0.88	0.89	0	0.88	
Kappa					0.76

Table 3. Confusion matrix generated for aggregated classes including shadows.

.Class	Impervious	Permeable	Shadows	Total	UA	**Kappa**
Impervious	88	10	0	98	0.90	
Permeable	12	77	0	89	0.87	
Shadows	11	2	0	13	0	
Total	111	89	0	200	0	
PA	0.8		0	0	0.83	
Kappa						0.67

4.3 Urban Landscape Metrics for Urban Land Use Pattern

SHDI was used to estimate the diversity of urban surfaces within user-defined polygons according to their physical characteristics (permeability). Based on the obtained SHDI values, the polygons are classified into five classes: 1) <0.2 (poor diversity), 2) 0.2–0.4 (slight), 3) 0.4–0.6 (moderate) 4) 0.6–0.8 (high) 5) 0.8–1.53 (very high) (Fig. 5). A high value of SHDI indicates that the types of land cover have approximately equal proportions. In contrast, a low value indicates that the landscape is dominated by one type of land cover) [22]. The absolute homogeneity (0) is not present within any of the polygons.

Of the total number of polygons 38.08% have a diversity greater than 0.8, and 27% poor, less than 0.2. Although there is no significant predominance of any class in the total area, their grouping in specific parts of the city is observed. At the edges of the city, polygons with permeable surfaces predominate, while impervious surfaces predominate in the inner-city parts. Polygons with a diversity higher than 0.8 coincide with the old city center and the wider area, which includes the residential zone (houses and buildings), and industrial and commercial zone (Fig. 5.). The largest patch is impervious surfaces with a slight (13–25) or moderate LPI (25–40). It was noticed that the polygons with the lowest SHDI (> 0 < 0.2) were mostly located in the recreational zone, Marjan Forest Park. In this area, the predominant urban pattern is tree cover, and the LPI is higher than 65%. To better understand these patterns, we derived specific UPIs.

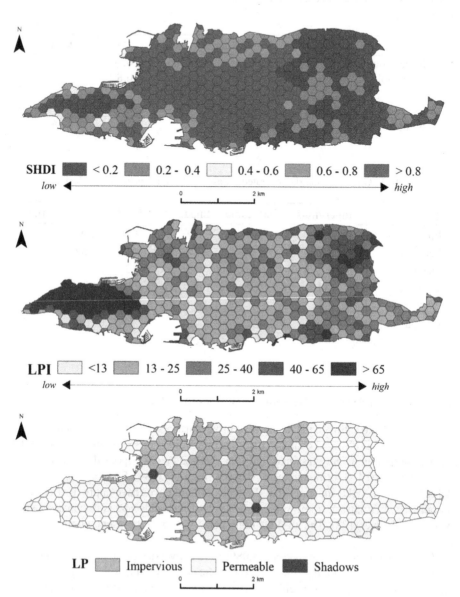

Fig. 5. Landscape metrics for city of Split (SHDI, LPI, LP).

4.4 Urban Planning Indicators (UPIs)

The derived UPIs (Fig. 6) showed that vegetation indicators have a higher percentage in the outskirts of the city, with the exception of the SK0109932 located in the western part of the city, dominated by the Marjan Forest Park which has the highest GCR among all circles (92.38%). Forest-Park is one of eleven nature protection categories in Croatia. Tree cover is making 85.72% of the SK0109932 [54]. The high GCR is also noticed in adjacent units south (SK0109959, SK0109908) of Marjan and in the eastern part (SK0110701) where GCR mostly consists of lawn cover (Fig. 6). This SK includes the Mejaši, a relatively young neighborhood that was merged with the city in the 2000s. In recent times new residential buildings have been constructed in this area. As expected, these statistical circles have the lowest ratio of impervious surfaces [54].

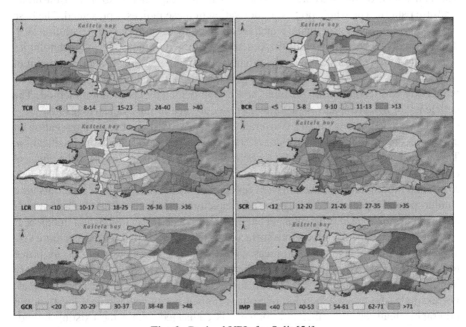

Fig. 6. Derived UPIs for Split [54].

The old city center along with the wider city center area stands out as the most built-up part. These units (SK0109827, SK0109860, SK0109843, SK0110205, SK0109894, etc.) are characterized by a prevalence of impervious surfaces (67–82%) and a lack of green areas. The most dominant type of impervious surfaces in this area are streets and buildings. These are older residential neighborhoods) [46]. The northern outskirts (SK 0110582, SK 0110655) of the city are also characterized by a high presence of impervious surfaces (Fig. 6). However, this part of the city is highly industrialized. Statistical circles characterized by the highest values of SCR (SK 0110205, SK 0110582, SK 0110060, SK 0110574, SK 0110655, SK 0110647) are located nearby the industrial zone, central bus station, and passenger port [54].

A large percentage of the IMP (buildings, roads, houses) in statistical circles is not surprising given the history of spatial-functional development of the Split settlement. Namely, in the period from the Second World War to the 1990s, housing construction in Split was marked by socially-oriented collective construction with the objective to build as many residential buildings as possible in the smallest area possible. After the intensified industrialization a process on the outskirts of the city, due to cheaper land, the construction of individual, mostly illegal housing units is taking place, which in the 1990s became the dominant form of housing construction) [46].

5 Conclusion

The main results of this study are performed urban-landscape metrics to analyze the urban land-use pattern. The whole process of derivation of these indices is presented. The base of analysis is the land cover model which is generated from the very-high-resolution WV-3 satellite imagery using the GEOBIA method. Although remote sensing technologies provide up-to-date information on the urban landscape in a relatively shorter amount of time it is necessary to emphasize that the generated final model is highly determined by the quality and resolution of MI input and by the depicted classification method. The deficiency of MS are shadows that affect the occurrence of false-negative results.

The Split land-cover model is overall moderately accurate but an aggregation of classes according to the physical characteristics increased the accuracy of classification. Therefore, for SHDI observation, we recommend classification according to the physical characteristics of the land cover rather than functionality. Although houses, buildings, roads, and other facilities have different functionalities they are made of materials with similar spectral signatures that may give a false picture of the heterogeneity of a particular area which can mislead urban planners and therefore lead to environmental imbalance.

The predominance of impervious surfaces can make certain parts of the city more vulnerable to various dangers. Urban areas with dominant impervious surfaces are prone to pluvial floods and the formation of thermal islands, so their identification is very important in urban planning. This is emphasized in cities with limited expansion areas. For example, the urban expansion of Split is limited by its geographical location and orographic features so further development is envisaged within the existing boundaries which will potentially affect the increase of imperviousness. Diversity analysis of hexagons showed that Split settlement is generally heterogeneous, and there are no polygons with only one type of LC. Still, domination of the impervious surfaces is noticeable in the city center and wider area. In that contest, metrics provided in this study can form a basis for future planning and spatial organization of the Split settlement. The UPIs values at the studied level are the reflection of the historical spatial-functional development and can be used for the analysis of different issues in an urban environment.

Acknowledgments. This work has been supported by INTERREG Italy- Croatia PEPSEA (Protecting the Enclosed Parts of the Sea in Adriatic from pollution) and the Croatian Science Foundation under the project UIP-2017-05-2694.

References

1. Liu, Y.: Modelling Urban Development with Geographical Information Systems and Cellular Automata. CRC Press (2009)
2. Du, S., Shi, P., Van Rompaey, A., Wen, J.: Quantifying the impact of impervious surface location on flood peak discharge in urban areas. Nat. Hazards **76**(3), 1457 (2015)
3. Wang, Z., et al.: Impact of rapid urbanization on the threshold effect in the relationship between impervious surfaces and water quality in Shanghai, China. Environ. Pollut., 115569 (2020)
4. Petralli, M., Massetti, L., Brandani, G., Orlandini, S.: Urban planning indicators: useful tools to measure the effect of urbanization and vegetation on summer air temperatures. Int. J. Climatol. **34**(4), 1236–1244 (2014)
5. Sleavin, W.J., Civco, D.L., Prisloe, S., Giannotti, L.: Measuring impervious surfaces for non-point source pollution modeling. In: Proceedings of the ASPRS 2000 Annual Conference, pp. 22–26, May 2000
6. Sinha, B.R.K. (ed.): Multidimensional Approach to Quality of Life Issues (2019)
7. Watson, V.: 'The planned city sweeps the poor away...': urban planning and 21st century urbanization. Prog. Plan. **72**(3), 151–193 (2009)
8. Miller, R.B., Small, C.: Cities from space: potential applications of remote sensing in urban environmental research and policy. Environ. Sci. Policy **6**(2), 129–137 (2003)
9. Hall, P.G.: Urban and Regional Planning. 4 edn. (2002)
10. Anguluri, R., Narayanan, P.: Role of green space in urban planning: outlook towards smart cities. Urban For. Urban Greening **25**, 58–65 (2017)
11. Levy, J.M.: Contemporary Urban Planning. Taylor & Francis (2016)
12. Sénécal, G.: Urban environment: mapping a concept. Introductory note. Environ. Urbain Urban Environ. **1** (2007)
13. Blaschke, T., Hay, G.J., Weng, Q., Resch, B.: Collective sensing: integrating geospatial technologies to understand urban systems—an overview. Remote Sens. **3**(8), 1743–1776 (2011)
14. Brownson, R.C., Hoehner, C.M., Day, K., Forsyth, A., Sallis, J.F.: Measuring the built environment for physical activity: state of the science. Am. J. Prev. Med. **36**(4), S99–S123 (2009)
15. Gong, Y., Palmer, S., Gallacher, J., Marsden, T., Fone, D.: A systematic review of the relationship between objective measurements of the urban environment and psychological distress. Environ. Int. **96**, 48–57 (2016)
16. Abbate, G., Fiumi, L., De Lorenzo, C., Vintila, R.: Evaluation of remote sensing data for urban planning. Applicative examples by means of multispectral and hyperspectral data. In: 2nd GRSS/ISPRS Joint Workshop on 2003 Remote Sensing and Data Fusion over Urban Areas (2003)
17. Tenedório, J.A., Rebelo, C., Estanqueiro, R., Henriques, C.D., Marques, L., Gonçalves, J.A.: New developments in geographical information technology for urban and spatial planning. In: Geospatial Research: Concepts, Methodologies, Tools, and Applications, pp. 1965–1997. IGI Global (2016)
18. Bodzin, A.M., Cirucci, L.: Integrating geospatial technologies to examine urban land-use change: a design partnership. J. Geogr. **108**(4–5), 186–197 (2009)
19. Marić, I., Šiljeg, A., Domazetović, F.: Geoprostorne tehnologije u 3D dokumentaciji i promociji kulturne baštine–primjer utvrde Fortica na otoku Pagu. Geodetski glasnik **50**, 19–44 (2019)
20. Dibiase, D., et al.: Geographic Information Science & technology: body of knowledge. USGIS, Association of American Geographers, Washington, DC (2006)

21. Dimoudi, A., Nikolopoulou, M.: Vegetation in the urban environment: microclimatic analysis and benefits. Energy Build. **35**(1), 69–76 (2003)
22. LeGates, R., Tate, N.J., Kingston, R.: Spatial thinking and scientific urban planning. Environ. Plann. B. Plann. Des. **36**(5), 763–768 (2009)
23. McGarigal, K., Cushman, S.A., Neel, M.C., Ene, E.: FRAGSTATS: Spatial Pattern Analysis Program for Categorical Maps, project homepage, University of Massachusetts, Amherst (2002)
24. Vivoni, E.R., Teles, V., Ivanov, V.Y., Bras, R.L., Entekhabi, D.: Embedding landscape processes into triangulated terrain models. Int. J. Geogr. Inf. Sci. **19**(4), 429–457 (2005)
25. Schindler, S., Poirazidis, K., Wrbka, T.: Towards a core set of landscape metrics for biodiversity assessments: a case study from Dadia National Park, Greece. Ecol. Ind. **8**(5), 502–514 (2008). https://doi.org/10.1016/j.ecolind.2007.06.001
26. Uuemaa, E., Antrop, M., Roosaare, J., Marja, R., Mander, Ü.: Landscape metrics and indices: an overview of their use in landscape research. Living Rev. Landscape Res. **3**(1), 1–28 (2009)
27. Aghsaei, H., et al.: Effects of dynamic land use/land 1039 cover change on water resources and sediment yield in the Anzali wetland catchment, Gilan, Iran. Sci. Total Environ. **712**, 136449 (2020). https://doi.org/10.1016/j.scitotenv.2019.136449
28. Horning, N.: Reference module in earth systems and environmental sciences. Remote Sens. (2018). https://doi.org/10.1016/B978-0-12-409548-9.10607-4
29. Wang, Z., Gang, C., Li, X., Chen, Y., Li, J.: Application of a normalized difference impervious index (NDII) to extract urban impervious surface features based on Landsat TM images. Int. J. Remote Sens. **36**(4), 1055–1069 (2015)
30. Zhao, C., Fu, G., Liu, X., Fu, F.: Urban planning indicators, morphology and climate indicators: a case study for a north–south transect of Beijing, China. Build. Environ. **46**, 1174–1183 (2011)
31. Lin, P., Lau, S.S.Y., Qin, H., Gou, Z.: Effects of urban planning indicators on urban heat island: a case study of pocket parks in high-rise high-density environment. Landsc. Urban Plan. **168**, 48–60 (2017)
32. Shen, L.Y., Ochoa, J.J., Shah, M.N., Zhang, X.: The application of urban sustainability indicators–a comparison between various practices. Habitat Int. **35**(1), 17–29 (2011)
33. La Rosa, D.: Accessibility to greenspaces: GIS based indicators for sustainable planning in a dense urban context. Ecol. Ind. **42**, 122–134 (2014)
34. Chrysoulakis, N., et al.: A conceptual list of indicators for urban planning and management based on earth observation. ISPRS Int. J. Geo Inf. **3**(3), 980–1002 (2014)
35. Bryant, M.M.: Urban landscape conservation and the role of ecological greenways at local and metropolitan scales. Landsc. Urban Plan. **76**(1–4), 23–44 (2006)
36. Elshater, A.: Widen the scale of urban design to the level of city planning: argument beyond a case of two cities. UPLanD-J. Urban Plann. Landscape Environ. Des. **2**(2), 207–221 (2017)
37. Hay, G.J., Castilla, G.: Geographic object-based image analysis (GEOBIA): a new name for a new discipline. In: Blaschke, T., Lang, S., Hay, G.J. (eds.) Object-Based Image Analysis, pp. 75–89. Springer, Heidelberg (2008). https://doi.org/10.1007/978-3-540-77058-9_4
38. Šiljeg, S., Marić, I., Nikolić, G., Šiljeg, A.: Accessibility analysis of urban green spaces in the settlement of Zadar in Croatia. Šumarski list **142**(9–10), 487–496 (2018)
39. Ye, B., Tian, S., Ge, J., Sun, Y.: Assessment of WorldView-3 data for lithological mapping. Remote Sens. **9**(11), 1132 (2017)
40. Maxar Technologies: Stereo Imagery datasheet (2019). https://www.digitalglobe.com/resources. Accessed 03 Dec 2020
41. Bhakti, T., et al.: Combining land cover, animal behavior, and master plan regulations to assess landscape permeability for birds. Landsc. Urban Plan. **214**, 104171 (2021)

42. Zhan, Q., Shi, W., Xiao, Y.: Quantitative analysis of shadow effects in high-resolution images of urban areas. In: International Archives of Photogrammetry and Remote Sensing, vol. 36, no. 8/W27 (2005)

43. Zhang, P., Ke, Y., Zhang, Z., Wang, M., Li, P., Zhang, S.: Urban land use and land cover classification using novel deep learning models based on high spatial resolution satellite imagery. Sensors **18**(11), 3717 (2018)

44. Foody, G.M.: Explaining the unsuitability of the kappa coefficient in the assessment and comparison of the accuracy of thematic maps obtained by image classification. Remote Sens. Environ. **239**, 111630 (2020). https://doi.org/10.1016/j.rse.2019.111630

45. Fleiss, J.L., Levin, B., Paik, M.C.: Statistical Methods for Rates and Proportions. Wiley (2013)

46. Myint, S.W., Gober, P., Brazel, A., Grossman-Clarke, S., Weng, Q.: Per-pixel vs. object-based classification of urban land cover extraction using high spatial resolution imagery **115**(5), 1145–1161 (2011). https://doi.org/10.1016/j.rse.2010.12.017

47. Klempić, S.: Razvoj stambenih naselja Splita nakon Drugog svjetskog rata. Hrvatski geografski glasnik **66**(2), 95–119 (2004)

48. Kranjčić, N., Medak, D., Župan, R., Rezo, M.: Machine learning methods for classification of the green infrastructure in city areas. ISPRS Int. J. Geo Inf. **8**(10), 463 (2019)

49. Chen, W., Li, X., Wang, L.: Fine land cover classification in an open pit mining area using optimized support vector machine and WorldView-3 imagery. Remote Sens. **12**(1), 82 (2019)

50. Hiscock, O.H., Back, Y., Kleidorfer, M., Urich, C.: A GIS-based land cover classification approach suitable for fine-scale urban water management. Water Resour. Manage **35**(4), 1339–1352 (2021)

51. Benarchid, O., Raissouni, N.: Mean-shift segmentation parameters estimator (MSPE): a new tool for very high spatial resolution satellite images. In: 2014 International Conference on Multimedia Computing and Systems (ICMCS), pp. 357–361. IEEE, April 2014

52. Choi, J., Park, H., Seo, D.: Pansharpening using guided filtering to improve the spatial clarity of VHR satellite imagery. Remote Sens. **11**(6), 633 (2019)

53. Rwanga, S.S., Ndambuki, J.M.: Accuracy assessment of land use/land cover classification using remote sensing and GIS. Int. J. Geosci. **8**(04), 611 (2017)

54. Nagendra, H.: Opposite trends in response for the Shannon and Simpson indices of landscape diversity **22**(2), 0–186 (2002). https://doi.org/10.1016/s0143-6228(02)00002-4

55. Milošević, R., Šiljeg, S., Marić, I.: Derivation of urban planning indicators (UPIs) using Worldview-3 imagery and GEOBIA method for split settlement, Croatia. In: Proceedings of the 7th International Conference on Geographical Information Systems Theory, Applications and Management, pp. 267–273 (2021). ISBN 978-989-758-503-6, ISSN 2184-500X. https://doi.org/10.5220/0010465102670273

Potential and Limitations of Free Online Precise Point Positioning Services for GNSS Rover-Base Surveys in Low-Density CORS Areas

Elena Belcore[1]($\boxtimes$) (iD), Marco Piras[1] (iD), Paolo Dabove[1] (iD), Giovanni Massazza[2] (iD),
and Maurizio Rosso[1] (iD)

[1] DIATI, Department of Environment, Land and Infrastructure Engineering, Politecnico di
Torino, 10129 Turin, Italy
{elena.belcore,marco.piras,paolo.dabove,
maurizio.rosso}@polito.it
[2] Agenzia Interregionale Per Il Fiume Po (AIPo), 10024 Moncalieri, Italy
giovanni.massazza@agenziapo.it

Abstract. In the last years, the diffusion of the Precise Point Positioning (PPP) technique has constantly increased thanks to the more precise and accurate results that it can reach. Until some years ago, this technique was limited by long measurement sessions to obtain good precisions (centimetre-level), using only one GNSS dual frequency receiver. Online PPP free services that permit broad access to PPP technique have spread. In this contribution, two PPP online services (Canadian Spatial Reference System Precise Point Positioning tool; Automatic Precise Positioning Service) are analysed as potential solutions for realising GNSS surveys in disadvantaged areas for the lack of geodetic infrastructures. The PPP online services are compared with a relative positioning online tool (AUSPOS). Their elaboration power was tested for different stationing times (three scenarios of 3 h, 1 h and 30 min, respectively). The data PPP-treated were collected in southwest Niger, along the Sirba river. The results reveal precisions and relative accuracies lower than 5 cm for three hours sessions. The short observation sessions (i.e. one hour and half hour) emerged that APPS provide the most confident solutions. The less performant service is AUSPOS, which provides 0,612 cm precision for one hour. CSRS-PPP has precision values between the ones of AUSPOS and APPS.

Keywords: Point Positioning · High-Precision GNSS · NRTK · Free and Open Services · Sub-Saharan Africa · Niger · Sirba River · Sahel · Topographic Survey · Geodetic Disadvantaged Areas

1 Introduction

In recent years, the Global Navigation Satellite System (GNSS) has overcome traditional survey methods, becoming a standard tool in many surveying sectors. Nowadays, GNSS systems play a lead role in data acquisition thanks to the increasing number of satellites, the low cost, the efficiency, and the variety of available products. From 2002 forward [1],

Real-Time Kinematic networks (NRTK) have spread. These networks are composed of GNSS stations of known coordinates, called Continuously Operating Reference Stations (CORS), and managed by network software installed in a control centre. The introduction of the CORSs has allowed users to collect data using one GNSS multi-frequency receiver (instead of two). This is possible thanks to the direct connection between the CORS and the dual-frequency receiver through the control centre. Today, a dense world network of permanent stations to process GNSS data exists [2], revolutionising the data acquisition modalities [3, 4].

Although CORSs cover most of the world's countries today, some areas are still not included in the network, such as some sub-Saharan countries (Fig. 1). Considering the real-time positioning and the NRTK method, the rover receiver must be within a short distance (less than 60 km) from the reference stations [5, 6].

A short baseline is fundamental to minimise the distance-dependent errors induced by the troposphere, the ionosphere, and the orbital errors [7]. This specific requirement can be an obstacle to realising NRTK surveys where there are no CORS within hundreds of kilometres [8]. A possibility to overcome the lack of CORS is resorting to two GNSS dual-frequency receivers in the rover-base modality. This data collection method requires two GNSS receivers to communicate with each other (usually via radio): one works as "base" or "master" (substituting the permanent station) and the other as "rover" that collects the coordinates of the points of interest for the survey. The coordinates of the base station must be known.

When a known-coordinates point is unavailable, post-processing operations are compulsory to obtain the base's correct position. One of the most common post-processing methods is the PPP (Precise Point Positioning). To perform it, data regarding satellites' orbits and the ionosphere are needed to process the pseudo-range and carrier phase measures of GNSS multi-frequency receivers [9–11]. These data are collected by permanent stations that can also be located very far from the surveyed area [10]. In terms of East, North, and Up components, the PPP can provide centimetre-level precisions in static mode [12, 13] if the phase ambiguities are correctly fixed as integer values [14, 15]. The precision of PPP corrections depends on the measurement session's duration [16, 17]. Its effectiveness for the estimation of the positions has been demonstrated by several authors, e.g. [10, 11, 18, 19], using precise orbits and satellite clocks from IGS [20, 21] and many other providers [17, 22, 23]. RTK is a relative positioning technique based on carrier-phase. A minimum of four shared satellites between the two receivers is required. Tracking more than four satellites improves the GPS position solution's precision and allows it to obtain a sub-centimetre accuracy level. The excellent accuracy results are also because errors and bias from the same satellite should be equal. Thus, shorter is the baseline, and more similar are the errors. Several error sources affecting positioning accuracy in GNSS surveys exist [24]. Today relative technique provides better solutions than the PPP technique in terms of accuracy [25]. The primary reason is the lower effects of satellite orbit errors over relative techniques than the PPP technique.

Moreover, relative techniques can eliminate clock errors using double differencing phase measurements [26]. The primary error sources of PPP (such as ionospheric and tropospheric delay and clock bias) are usually mitigated by: i) employing the combinations of dual-frequency GNSS measurements to eliminate the first-order ionospheric delay [10, 25]; ii) applying external error correction data (including satellite orbit and clock corrections); and iii) modelling the tropospheric delay to correct it. Since a part of tropospheric delay cannot be efficiently modelled because of its high variability, it is estimated (wet component of tropospheric delay). Precise satellite orbit and clock information are used to calculate the tropospheric residuals and associated gradients with proper stochastic models, which means that the estimates are constrained by the prior variance and its propagation value. Thus, PPP depends on the accuracy level of this information [25].

Fig. 1. CORS in north Africa. The blue dots indicate the stations that provide observations to the International GNSS Service (IGS), while the red square is the study area. Data Source: International GNSS Service (IGS), (https://www.igs.org/). (Color figure online)

Though RTK and PPP techniques provide similar precision and accuracy, they require different setups. On the one hand, RTK needs a complex configuration and (generally) expensive equipment, but it rapidly provides higher accuracy. It is worth remembering that the base station must be placed precisely on a known-coordinate point to achieve high accuracy. On the other hand, the PPP technique needs a more straightforward setup, but it has lower accuracy and a longer initial convergence time [25, 26]. Also, since PPP does not use a base station, it is not affected by baseline length bias and can provide full accuracy anywhere in the world.

Until some years ago, the satellites' data, the ionosphere information, and the specific software necessary to perform PPP were not easily obtainable. The PPP was limited to a few expert users, such as academia and research institutes. Today, some commercial and scientific solutions to perform PPP exist (e.g., Bernese, GIPSY, and GAMIT). Such software can efficiently perform PPP as long as infrastructures with adequate computational power and skilled users are available. The PPP technique has raised the attention of academia, industry, and governments [9]. In particular, the last ones have dedicated specific attention to PPP, and some shared the socio-economic benefits of PPP with the public, providing ad hoc coordinates online estimation services [9]. Some governmental research centres provide PPP online free services. It is sufficient to upload the GNSS raw data to obtain the correct position data from the services. These free web solutions for PPP do not require high computational power or exceptionally skilled users, but each service uses its estimation algorithms. Thus, the results provided can be very different.

The scientific literature offers some interesting analysis of PPP online services, where known coordinates points are processed with various PPP online services [27–29], and the estimated coordinates are compared with known ones. Nevertheless, as far as the authors know, few of these studies analyse data collected in geodetic disadvantaged areas. Indeed, the lack of CORS and known coordinates points is quite a frequent condition in sub-Saharan rural regions, strongly affecting topographic surveys.

This work compares two PPP online free services to correct RTK data collected through rover-base modality (i.e., static mode) in low-density CORS areas. The PPP services considered are the Canadian Spatial Reference System Precise Point Positioning tool (CSRS-PPP) and the Automatic Precise Positioning Service (APPS). A CORS-based post-processing free service is considered in the analysis as a non-PPP post-processing online tool: the AUSPOS Online GPS processing service (AUSPOS). The precision, the convergence time (meant as the length of time required to reach centimetre-level positional solutions), and the structure and condition of the services' use are analysed in this paper. The data used for the comparison were collected in February 2018 along the Sirba River (southwest Niger) in the framework of the ANADIA 2.0 project[1] and this work is premised on the outcomes of the tests that have been presented in [30].

2 The Case Study

ANADIA 2.0 project was born in 2017 to develop an early warning system against floods and strengthen the local technicians' competencies in monitoring and forecasting river floods [31]. Indeed, Sahelian floods have become a relevant issue in the last decades due to the ongoing climatic and land use changes [32, 33]. In this framework, high-precision surface and hydraulic numerical models are necessary as inputs for the development of forecast flood models [34–36]. Hence, to meet the project's data requirements, a topographic survey was carried out on the Middle Niger River Basin's main tributary, the Sirba River. More than 100 cross-sections were measured along a reach of 108 km (one section per km), and flood-risked-exposed infrastructures were measured during the dry period (February) to take advantage of the intermittent flow [37, 38]. 10 cm accuracy for the Up component was required [31].

Although the closest CORS to the study area are in Nigeria and Ivory Coast, they are more than 900 km away from the study region.

As discussed in the previous section, 900 km is a too-long baseline to guarantee centimetre accuracy. Besides, the closest known-coordinates points are around 200 km from the surveyed area. Considering these conditions, the only feasible way to collect data was an RTK survey in master-rover modality with a radio-modem connection. The PPP technique was used to post-process the data and estimate the base stations' coordinates. The data were collected with two STONEX S10 dual-frequency receivers.

---

[1] ANADIA 2.0 (Adaptation to climate change, disaster prevention and agricultural development for food security) is a project funded by the Italian Agency for Development Cooperation (AICS) and executed by Institute of BioEconomy of the National Research Council of Italy (IBE-CNR) in partnership with the Department of Regional and Urban Studies and Planning of the Politecnico di Torino (DIST) and the National Directorate for Meteorology of Niger (DMN).

The master receiver was placed in 17 stations along the Sirba River (Fig. 2), and 3,150 points were measured with the rover receiver. Each master station acquired data for at least two hours, considering a session length of 3 h and 22 min as maximum. GPS, GLONASS, BEIDOU and SBAS constellations were tracked.

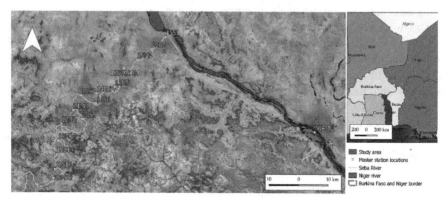

Fig. 2. Surveyed area of Sirba River basin. The yellow squares identify the locations of the stations along the river.

Some instruments malfunctioning, attributed to the high temperature, slowed down the data collection. In the hottest hours of the day, the temperature reached 40 °C, and the master receiver often overheated and stopped communication with the rover receiver. The communication happened via radio using RTCM communication protocol at 410–470 MHz frequency. The overheating prevented acquisition longer than 3 h for most of the stations. The receivers' communication was even more limited by the local topography (Fig. 3) and the abundant vegetation along the river. Regularly, if the receivers were more than 3 km away from each other, the communication stopped. In 9 days, 103 cross-sections along a river reach of 108 km were measured. The raw measurements were saved in the Receiver Independent Exchange Format (RINEX) 3.01 version with a sampling rate of 1 s.

3 Methodologies

As previously discussed, two possible techniques are available for post-processing: the phase-based relative solution (base-rover) or the PPP [6]. This paper will focus on the PPP approach [39]. Today many possibilities for obtaining PPP solutions from online services exist [40, 41]: some of them consider only the GPS constellation (e.g., APPS), and others ones also GLONASS satellites (CSRS-PPP). The data collected by the master receiver were stored in RINEX 3.01 version. Then, they were post-processed using two online PPP free services: i) The Canadian Spatial Reference System (CSRS-PPP) and ii) the Automatic Precise Positioning Service of the Global Differential GPS System (APPS). Additionally, data were processed using a relative positioning online service, iii) Online GPS Processing Service (AUSPOS), as a comparison against PPP technique geodetic disadvantaged areas. A summed table was created (Table 1) to recap the functioning of the three services.

Fig. 3. Environmental conditions during the survey activities in the field. The master receiver (on the tripod) is in the foreground, while the rover receiver is in the background.

3.1 Canadian Spatial Reference System Precise Point Positioning Tool (CSRS-PPP)

Operative since 2003, the CSRS-PPP is an online free tool provided by the Canadian Government [42]. It calculates the positions of the information collected by GNSS receivers with high accuracy based on the RINEX files [43].

The CSRS-PPP uses GNSS ephemerides to produce absolute accuracy coordinates, meaning using accuracy values independent of the collection's location. The estimated coordinates are as much accurate as long in the acquisition session. The CSRS-PPP uses IGS ephemerides of three types, Final, Rapid, and Ultra Rapid that have the following accuracy values [44]:

- FINAL (±2 cm), available after 13–15 days from the acquisition day, from the end of the data collection week.
- RAPID (±5 cm), available from the day after the data collection.
- ULTRA RAPID (±15 cm), available every 90 min.

The service can process data in Kinematic and Static modes. Data can be post-processed inNAD83 (inserting the referring epoch) or ITRF (International Terrestrial Reference Frame) reference systems. It is possible to automatically convert ellipsoid height into orthometric height by choosing between CGDV28 (Canadian Geodetic Vertical Datum of 1928) or CGDV2013 (Canadian Geodetic Vertical Datum of 2013), both valid only for surveys realised in Canada. It is possible to upload an Ocean Tidal Loading (OTL) file. The results are sent by email.

3.2 Automatic Precise Positioning Service (APPS)

The APPS is an online free service provided by the Jet Propulsion Laboratory (JPL) of the California Institute of Technology of USA National Aeronautics and Space Administration (NASA). Its elaboration is based on the Global Differential GPS System (GDGPS) products of JPL and the software GIPSY-OASIS developed by JPL. It applies a broad and spread geodetic structure (more than 200 stations distributed worldwide). The GDGPS operates since 2000 and declares a 99.999% reliability and precision under 10 cm [45]. The APPS uses the Jet Propulsion Laboratory's final products of three types: Final, Rapid, and Ultra Rapid Real-time [45]. The declared accuracy values are:

- FINAL ($\pm$3cm), called FlinnR, are available after ten days from the acquisition day.
- RAPID ($\pm$5 cm), called QuickLookR), are available the day after the data collection.
- ULTRA RAPID ($\pm$8 cm), 1 min after data is collected.

Registration is compulsory to have full access to the service. The available options for the PPP are the processing mode (static or kinematic); the L1 code (C/A or P), if an atmospheric pressure model is requested (it can be helpful in the calculation of the hydrostatic delay for the troposphere modelling), the type of weight to assign to the elevation datum (flat, sin or sqrt). The advanced options allow the user to set the value of the cut-off angle and the output rate in seconds (clearly available only for kinematic surveys). 10 Mb is the maximum file size allowed, and the files must be in RINEX version 2.x. The results are provided directly in the upload window.

3.3 AUSPOS Online GPS Processing Service

It is an online free service provided by the Australian Government. It uses the relative positioning technique to estimate the coordinate of an unknown-positioned mark when it is over a reference station of known coordinates [23]. The Bernese Software System, used to correct the coordinates, is very rigorous in the definition of orbital parameters, and everything concerns the modelling of the geodetic aspects [46]. IGS provides the information and the parameters regarding the orbit and the Earth's orientation. Like the CSRS-PPP and APPS, it uses the best available ephemerides. It is fundamental to underline that AUSPOS does not provide a PPP service since the applied data correction uses data of the nearest IGS and Asia Pacific Reference Frame (APREF) stations. Consequentially, the data confidence and the time dependency are influenced by the distance of the reference stations used for the coordinates estimation. It was included in this analysis as representative of the relative positioning of online free tools. The service does not require any registration. The only information needed for the elaboration is the model, the antenna height, and an email address. The files must be in RINEX version 2.11. The upload limit is 20 files at once, but data must be referred for seven days. AUSPOS sends the results via email.

Table 1. Summary of the main characteristics of the three services at the processing time, calculated on a 10 Mb file. *If users submit RINEX V3 file, C2S (code measurement) and L2S (phase measurement) from L2 frequency will NOT be accepted as presented in [30].

	CSRS-PPP	APPS	AUSPOS
RINEX version	3.x	2.x	2.11*
Maximum file size	300 Mb	10 Mb	Not specified
Multi-file upload	Yes	Yes	Only via FTP
FTP	No	Yes	Yes
Height of the antenna	Automatically detected	Automatically detected	Manually set
User-defined elevation-dependent data weighted	No	Yes	No
User-defined cut-off angle	No (default 7.5)	Yes	No
L1 code	Yes	Yes	No
Upload of pressure model	No	Yes	No
Direct results	No	Yes	No
Compulsory registration to the website	Yes	No	No
Processing time (minutes)*	20	3	20
Reference system(s) of the results	ITRF 2014, NAD83	ITRF 2014	ITRF 2014
Orthometric heights	Yes	No	Yes
Elaboration report	Yes	No	Yes
Graphic restitution of the elaboration statistics	Yes	No	Yes
Ambiguity resolution	No	Yes	Yes
GNSS constellations processed	GPS+GLONASS	GPS	GPS

4   Results and Discussion

Before the PPP processing, the RINEX data were pre-processed. The RINEX files version 3 were converted into RINEX version 2.11 with the RTKCONV tool that is part of the open source software RTKLIB (http://www.rtklib.com/) [47]. Furthermore, the frequency rate of acquisition was reduced to one observation every 5 s to have files of less than 10 Mb, which is the file size limit of APPS service. The analysis considers the precisions of the estimation of each service and the relative accuracy (measured as the difference between coordinates) of 17 stations (one station of ANADIA 2.0 was excluded from this analysis because it is located outside the Sirba River basin). The final coordinates have been converted into WGS84/UTM31N coordinates system. The APPS service provides the σ values with 68% confidence, while CSRS-PPP and AUSPOS calculate 95% uncertainties. Therefore, the uncertainty values of APPS were related to 2σ confidence. Table 2 shows the session length and the date of acquisition for each station.

Table 2. Characteristics of the positions of the master receivers (Stations) analyzed in [30] and resumed in this work. Gr = group, *dd/mm/yyyy.

Station ID	Date of acquisition*	Starting time	Ending time	Session length	Gr
12S2	12/02/2018	12:58	14:49	01:51	1
10S4	10/02/2018	15:08	17:07	01:59	
14M6	14/02/2018	09:28	11:43	02:15	
10M4	10/02/2018	10:28	12:54	02:26	
15S1	15/02/2018	13:46	16:30	02:44	2
19S14	19/01/2018	14:02	16:49	02:47	
20S9	20/01/2018	14:24	17:12	02:48	
15M3	15/01/2018	08:17	11:08	02:51	
18S16	18/01/2018	14:09	17:02	02:53	
21M8	21/01/2018	08:53	11:46	02:53	
14S6	14/01/2018	13:38	16:35	02:57	
11M5	11/01/2018	09:05	12:05	03:00	
11S7	11/01/2018	13:43	16:52	03:09	3
12M2	12/01/2018	08:50	12:05	03:15	
18M18	18/01/2018	08:05	11:28	03:23	
20M12	20/01/2018	08:45	12:09	03:24	
19M14	19/01/2018	08:25	11:52	03:27	
12S2	12/02/2018	12:58	14:49	01:51	

For the analysis, the stations were distributed in three groups of uniform acquisition length: *group 1* less than 2,5 h acquisition length; *group 2* between 2,5 and 3 h; and *group 3* more than 3 h. The CSRS-PPP values had been taken as a reference for comparing the services, as shown in Eqs. 1 and 2.

$$\Delta CSRS\text{-}APPS = EC\_CSRS\text{-}EC\_APPS \qquad (1)$$

$$\Delta CSRS\text{-}AUSPOS = EC\_CSRS\text{-}EC\_AUSPOS \qquad (2)$$

Where *EC_ CSRS* are the North, East and Ellipsoidal height coordinates of each sample point estimated by CSRS; *EC_ APPS* are the North, East and Ellipsoidal height coordinates of each sample point estimated by APPS; *EC_ AUSPOS* are the North, East and Ellipsoidal height coordinates of each sample point estimated by AUSPOS. According to [48], a minimum of one hour is required for the horizontal solution from a standard PPP static processing to converge to 5 cm. Approximately 20 min are needed for 95% of solutions to reach a horizontal accuracy of 20 cm [49]. Thus, three different scenarios of time acquisition were created using RTKLIBCONV [47] to investigate the effectiveness of the services on short acquisition time: full acquisition length, one hour, and a half-hour session.

Table 3 presents the minimum, maximum and average values of Δ CSRS-APPS and ΔCSRS-AUSPOS, calculated as illustrated in Eqs. 1 and 2.

Table 3. Minimum, Maximum, and Average of the differences between the coordinates estimated by CSRS, APPS, and AUSPOS for each station as reported by [30].

Gr			Min	Max	Av
1	Δ CSRS-APPS	East	0.007	0.019	0.014
		North	0.008	0.014	0.011
		Up	0.005	0.046	0.024
	Δ CSRS-AUSPOS	East	0.005	0.067	0.023
		North	0.001	0.014	0.007
		Up	0.018	0.046	0.032
2	Δ CSRS-APPS	East	0.001	0.026	0.01
		North	0.002	0.011	0.006
		Up	0.006	0.037	0.016
	Δ CSRS-AUSPOS	East	0.001	0.013	0.008
		North	0.002	0.005	0.003
		Up	0.006	0.069	0.029
3	Δ CSRS-APPS	East	0.003	0.029	0.016
		North	0.001	0.008	0.003
		Up	0.001	0.024	0.011
	Δ CSRS-AUSPOS	East	0.000	0.04	0.021
		North	0.002	0.004	0.003
		Up	0.006	0.031	0.017

The difference between CSRS and AUSPOS of the East component ranges between 0 cm and 6.7 cm, which is a clue of high data dispersion. This is particularly evident from distances between the average values of Groups 1 and 2, and it clearly indicates the importance of stationing time longer than 1 h for improved precision. On the contrary, the North component of the Δ CSRS-AUSPOS (and the Δ CSRS-APPS, too) is more stable.

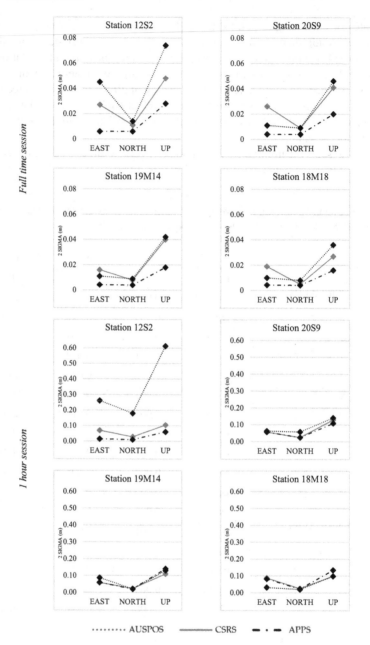

Fig. 4. Graphical analysis of the uncertainties values of East, North, and Up coordinates of the three services, obtained considering the full acquisition time and 1-h acquisition time [30].

Regarding the coordinates' precision, the calculated uncertainty values range from 0.2 cm (East and North of APPS) to 65 cm (Up component of AUSPOS). The latter is not representative of the analysis and was interpreted as an exceptional event; thus, it was excluded from the average computation. For AUSPOS, the distance from the reference CORS is crucial in estimating the coordinate. The baseline ranges from 500 km to 1500 km on 14 reference stations in these analyses. From the reference literature, we aspect Root Mean Square (RMS) values of position errors for baseline around 500 km less than 4 cm, and less than 6 cm on each component (E, N, U) for baseline more than 1000 km. Such values are calculated over 24 h of acquisitions [50]. For shorter stationing time, the precisions fall.

According to the report by Novatel [51], we can expect around 10 cm RMS values of the position errors for baseline lengths between 700 km and 1000 km in 3-h stationing. These values reflect our measures: AUSPOS is closed 8 cm on the Up component. For groups 1 and 2, the uncertainties on the East component estimated by APPS are slightly lower than those of other services (Fig. 3). Figure 3 shows the graphical analysis of the uncertainty values of the East, North, and Up components and considers the full and 1-h acquisition time. Similarly to Table 3, what stands out in Fig. 3 is the decrease in uncertainties from Full-time acquisition (Group 3) and one-hour sessions (Group 1) (Fig. 5).

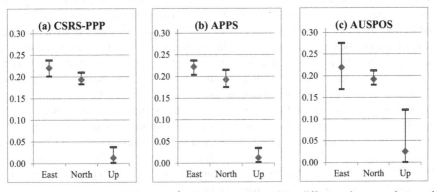

Fig. 5. Average (square), Minimum and Maximum values of the difference between the coordinates estimated by online post-processing services and the real coordinates. Average, minimum, and maximum are calculated for AUSPOS (a), CSRS (b), and APPS (c) in [30].

CSRS-PPP and APPS provide the lowest uncertainty values. With a shorter acquisition time, the confidence levels of CSRS-PPP and APPS get closer (Fig. 3), while AUSPOS shows similar trends for some stations (i.e., 19M14 and 18M18) and very different for others (station 12S2). Table 4 lists the difference values between the coordinates elaborated with the services on the 1-h session. Even if these trends are similar to full acquisitions, a significant distance between the Up components can be observed: the ΔCSRS-APPS peaks at 40 cm. For 30 min-acquisition time, AUSPOS did not provide any results because one hour is the minimum acquisition time required to perform the coordinates estimations. CSRS-PPP and APPS's performances peak in the East component of 20 cm and reach 50 cm on the Up component.

Table 4. Minimum, Maximum, and Average of the difference between the coordinates estimated by CSRS, APPS, and AUSPOS for each sample station (1 h session), [30].

Service	ITRF	One-hour session Δ (m)		
		Min	Max	Av
Δ CSRS-APPS	East	0.001	0.140	0.030
	North	0.000	0.374	0.032
	Up	0.005	0.108	0.044
Δ CSRS-AUSPOS	East	0.006	0.432	0.099
	North	0.002	0.403	0.037
	Up	0.033	0.286	0.165

5   Data Validation

The lack of CORS in Niger makes it challenging to test the accuracy of PPP services. Since there are no known-coordinates points to be used as a reference for accuracy analysis, only the precision values can be evaluated. To overcome this major constraint, we analysed accuracies of post-processing services solutions in sub-Saharan areas considering the data of CORS settled in countries close to Niger. CORS at the same latitude of the study area was sought to guarantee both the mean atmospheric conditions (ionospheric and tropospheric delays) and satellite geometry distribution. Another possible approach could be to collect 24 h of data to obtain results independent of the satellite geometry distribution and guarantee the solution's convergence, as described in the literature [52, 53]. However, it was impossible to realise long-session sessions due to weather conditions. Hence, to check the estimations' accuracy, raw observations of a CORS close to the surveyed area were analysed with online services. The selected CORS was the YKRO station (Yamoussoukro Tracking Station) in Cote d'Ivoire (1000 km away from the study area) and part of the IGS network (Table 5).

Table 5. Main characteristics of YKRO. Source: IGS website, [30].

YKRO Site Information	
City	Yamoussoukro
Country	Cote d'Ivoire
Tectonic Plate	African Plate
Approximate Position, DMS (ITRF)	LAT: +06°52′ 14.0170″ LON: −05°14′ 24.3347″
Elevation ellipsoid (m)	270.263
Date Installed	18-07-1999

This station was chosen because it is the closest station (considering latitude) to the investigated area, and it was operative at the time of the survey, February 2018. Besides, it is away from the sea. This may ensure atmosphere conditions as similar as possible to the ones in the study area. YKRO data of the survey days and the daily observations (12th of each month of 2018) were downloaded from the IGS website. The YKRO dataset was reduced to 3 h-lasting RINEX from 14.00 to 17.00, as the average lasting and representative time for Sirba River acquisitions. Data were processed with the online free services and estimated coordinated compared to the reference ones of the YKRO CORS (Table 5). The results show relatively constant performances for the North component and more dispersed results for the East and Up components. Figure 4 compares summary statistics (average, minimum and maximum values) for the differences calculated between real and estimated coordinates. The highest dispersion of the East component stands out in the graphs. CSRS and APPS have similar trends on the components, while AUSPOS, even if it has average values close to one of the PPP, provided varying results for the Up and East components. The results are never below 10 cm on the East and North components while reaching 1 cm on the Up component. According to the literature, we should obtain precision under 20 cm on horizontal components in 20 min. In our case, CSRS-PPP did not provide results under 20 cm in a half-hour on the East component. For example, in 30 min of session length, we reach the average precision of 0.247 cm on the East component. The results expected for one-hour sessions are approximately 5 cm on the horizontal component. APPS fits well these general rules on East and North components, while CSRS only focuses on the North component.

The coefficients of determination (R^2, listed in Table 6) confirm these observations. They verify that the estimated East component is the closest to the three services' reference values, reaching 0.737 for the CSRS-PPP service. AUSPOS records the most dispersed results in the Up component. In parallel, the Root Mean Square Error (RMSE) calculated over each service's estimations' position errors provides a view of the accuracy. The East component presents the highest values, followed by the North component. The lowest-RMSE service is the APPS for the Up component.

Table 6. R2 and RMSE values for the 2018 monthly dataset of solutions provided by the analysed services, [30].

R^2			
Online Service	East	North	Up
CSRS	0.235	0.737	0.273
AUSPOS	0.070	0.292	0.017
APPS	0.253	0.391	0.104
RMSE (m)			
CSRS	0.220	0.193	0.016
AUSPOS	0.221	0.192	0.040
APPS	0.223	0.193	0.015

Regarding YKRO analysis, even if remarkable differences between the coefficients of determination are present, the RMSE values differ for no more than 0.2 cm in the North and East components. The estimated height above the ellipsoid by APPS is the closest to the YKRO reference, only 1 mm on average values from CSRS-PPP. It is worth mentioning that AUSPOS does not use YKRO for ambiguity resolution, but it relies on stations located approximately 500–2000 km from YKRO.

CSRS-PPP and APPS use different ephemerids. This may affect the estimated coordinates because they strongly affect PPP results; thus, we might have different effects in the case of every other product. Besides this, the ephemerids seem not to interfere in the estimations. Additional considerations regarding the efficiency of PPP online free services can be addressed. APPS is the most rapid service in the data processing. It permits the analysis of a large quantity of data (industrial application) by uploading the RINEX files on an FTP provided by JPL (not tested in this contribution). APPS results are delivered directly from the website after a few seconds (depending on the data size), while AUSPOS and CSRS send the results via email. Nevertheless, APPS has an interface that may look complicated for non-GIPSY-expert users and does not provide the results in a report. CSRS-PPP is functional because the upload process is intuitive, and the results report is easily interpretable.

6 Conclusions

This manuscript tests and describes PPP online free services to correct RTK data collected through rover-base modality (i.e., static mode) in geodetic disadvantaged areas. Three GNSS post-processing services are analysed, the Canadian Spatial Reference System Precise Point Positioning tool (CSRS-PPP) and the Automatic Precise Positioning Service (APPS), and the AUSPOS Online GPS processing service (AUSPOS, CORS-based post-processing free service). The services are adequate and effective for the post-processing corrections of the master-rover RTK survey.

According to our analysis of Niger data, APPS reveals to be the most precise PPP free online service among the ones investigated in this paper, followed by CSRS-PPP, which guarantees satisfying performances in an easily interpretable report, and, finally, AUSPOS presents the less precise results, but it is highly intuitive.

The Canadian CSRS-PPP was used in the ANADIA 2.0 project. The obtained results have ± 4 cm precision, a value that satisfies the needs of the ANADIA II project in Niger. Nigerien technicians of the ministerial office in charge of meteorology and water resources have actively participated in the field surveys, appreciating the potential of the RTK master-rover survey.

References

1. Kamil, E., Turgut, U., Engin, G., Omer, Y., Ayhan, C.: Results from a comprehensive global navigation satellite system test in the CORS-TR network: case study. J. Surv. Eng. 135, 10–18 (2009). https://doi.org/10.1061/(ASCE)0733-9453(2009)135:1(10)
2. Kim, M., Seo, J., Lee, J.: A comprehensive method for GNSS data quality determination to improve ionospheric data analysis. Sensors 14, 14971–14993 (2014). https://doi.org/10.3390/s140814971

3. Grejner-Brzezinska, D.A., et al.: Efficiency and reliability of ambiguity resolution in network-based real-time kinematic GPS. J. Surv. Eng. **133**, 56–65 (2007). https://doi.org/10.1061/(ASC E)0733-9453(2007)133:2(56)

4. Rizos, C.: Alternatives to current GPS-RTK services and some implications for CORS infrastructure and operations. GPS Solutions **3**, 151–158 (2007). https://doi.org/10.1007/s10291-007-0056-x

5. Dabove, P., Cina, A., Manzino, A.M.: Single-frequency receivers as permanent stations in GNSS networks: precision and accuracy of positioning in mixed networks. In: Cefalo, R., Zieliński, J.B., Barbarella, M. (eds.) New Advanced GNSS and 3D Spatial Techniques. LNGC, pp. 101–109. Springer, Cham (2018). https://doi.org/10.1007/978-3-319-56218-6_8

6. Dabove, P., Manzino, A.M.: GPS & GLONASS mass-market receivers: positioning performances and peculiarities. Sensors **14**, 22159–22179 (2014). https://doi.org/10.3390/s14122 2159

7. El-Mowafy, A.: Precise Real-Time Positioning Using Network RTK. Global Navigation Satellite Systems: Signal, Theory and Applications (2012). https://doi.org/10.5772/29502

8. Elmezayen, A., El-Rabbany, A.: Precise point positioning using world's first dual-frequency GPS/GALILEO smartphone. Sensors **19**, 2593 (2019). https://doi.org/10.3390/s19112593

9. Bisnath, S., Gao, Y.: Current state of precise point positioning and future prospects and limitations. In: Sideris, M.G. (ed.) Proceedings of the Observing our Changing Earth, pp. 615–623. Springer, Heidelberg (2009). https://doi.org/10.1007/978-3-540-85426-5_71

10. Kouba, J., Héroux, P.: Precise point positioning using IGS orbit and clock products. GPS Solutions **5**, 12–28 (2001). https://doi.org/10.1007/PL00012883

11. Zumberge, J.F., Heflin, M.B., Jefferson, D.C., Watkins, M.M., Webb, F.H.: Precise point positioning for the efficient and robust analysis of GPS data from large networks. J. Geophys. Res. Solid Earth **102**, 5005–5017 (1997). https://doi.org/10.1029/96JB03860

12. Bisnath, S., Wells, D., Dodd, D.: Evaluation of Commercial Carrier-Phase-Based WADGPS Services for Marine Applications, pp. 17–27, 12 September 2003

13. Pan, S., Chen, W., Jin, X., Shi, X., He, F.: Real-time PPP based on the coupling estimation of clock bias and orbit error with broadcast ephemeris. Sensors **15**, 17808–17826 (2015). https://doi.org/10.3390/s150717808

14. Ge, M., Gendt, G., Rothacher, M., Shi, C., Liu, J.: Resolution of GPS carrier-phase ambiguities in precise point positioning (PPP) with daily observations. J. Geod. **82**, 389–399 (2008). https://doi.org/10.1007/s00190-007-0187-4

15. Collins, P., Bisnath, S.: Issues in Ambiguity Resolution for Precise Point Positioning, pp. 679–687, 23 September 2011

16. Yigit, C.O., Gikas, V., Alcay, S., Ceylan, A.: Performance evaluation of short to long term GPS, GLONASS and GPS/GLONASS post-processed PPP. Surv. Rev. **46**, 155–166 (2014). https://doi.org/10.1179/1752270613Y.0000000068

17. Mohammed, J., Bingley, R.M., Moore, T., Hill, C.: An Assessment of the Precise Products on Static Precise Point Positioning Using Multi-Constellation GNSS, pp. 634–641, 26 April 2018

18. Gao, Y., Shen, X.: A new method for carrier-phase-based precise point positioning. Navigation **49**, 109–116 (2002). https://doi.org/10.1002/j.2161-4296.2002.tb00260.x

19. Gao, Y., Harima, K., Shen, X.: Real-time kinematic positioning based on un-differenced carrier phase data processing. In: Proceedings of the Proceedings of the 2003 National Technical Meeting of The Institute of Navigation; Anaheim, CA, 22 January 2003, pp. 362–368 (2003)

20. Gao, Y., Chen, K.: Performance analysis of precise point positioning using rea-time orbit and clock products. Positioning (2004)

21. IGS IGS Network. http://www.igs.org/network. Accessed 4 Sept 2019

22. Wang, L., Li, Z., Ge, M., Neitzel, F., Wang, Z., Yuan, H.: Validation and assessment of multi-GNSS real-time precise point positioning in simulated kinematic mode using IGS real-time service. Remote Sensing **10**, 337 (2018). https://doi.org/10.3390/rs10020337

23. Marian, J., Gillins Daniel, T.: Comparative analysis of online static GNSS postprocessing services. J. Surv. Eng. **144**, 05018002 (2018). https://doi.org/10.1061/(ASCE)SU.1943-5428.0000256

24. Karaim, M., Elsheikh, M., Noureldin, A.: GNSS error sources. Multifunct. Oper. Appl. GPS (2018). https://doi.org/10.5772/intechopen.75493

25. Ocalan, T., et al.: Accuracy investigation of PPP method versus relative positioning using different satellite ephemerides products near/under forest environment. Earth Sci. Res. J. **20**, D1–D9 (2016). https://doi.org/10.15446/esrj.v20n4.59496

26. Nistor, S., Buda, A.S.: Ambiguity resolution in precise point positioning technique: a case study. J. Appl. Eng. Sci. **5**, 53–60 (2015). https://doi.org/10.1515/jaes-2015-0007

27. Arabi, M., Nankali, H.R.: Accuracy assessment of online PPP services in static positioning and Zenith Tropospheric Delay (ZTD) estimation. Geospat. Eng. J. **8**, 59–69 (2017)

28. Ozgur Uygur, S., Aydin, C., Demir, D.O., Cetin, S., Dogan, U.: Accuracy assessment for PPP by comparing various online PPP service solutions with Bernese 5.2 network solution, 18, EPSC2016-7102 (2016)

29. Oluyori, P.D., Ono, M.N., Okiemute, E.S.: Comparison of OPUS, CSRS-PPP and MagicGNSS Online Post-Processing Software of DGPS Observations for Geometric Geoid Modelling in FCT, Abuja. Social Science Research Network, Rochester (2019)

30. Belcore, E., Piras, M., Dabove, P., Massazza, G., Rosso, M.: Comparison of free and Open PPP services for master-base positioning in geodetic disadvantaged areas: case study along the Sirba River in Sub-Saharan Africa: In: Proceedings of the Proceedings of the 8th International Conference on Geographical Information Systems Theory, Applications and Management; SCITEPRESS - Science and Technology Publications: Online Streaming, --- Select a Country --- pp. 37–47 (2022)

31. Massazza, G., et al.: Flood hazard scenarios of the Sirba River (Niger): evaluation of the hazard thresholds and flooding areas. Water **11**, 1018 (2019). https://doi.org/10.3390/w11051018

32. Bigi, V., Pezzoli, A., Rosso, M.: Past and future precipitation trend analysis for the city of Niamey (Niger): an overview. Climate **6**, 73 (2018). https://doi.org/10.3390/cli6030073

33. Tamagnone, P., Massazza, G., Pezzoli, A., Rosso, M.: Hydrology of the Sirba River: updating and analysis of discharge time series. Water **11**, 156 (2019). https://doi.org/10.3390/w11010156

34. Tarchiani, V., et al.: Community and impact based early warning system for flood risk preparedness: the experience of the Sirba River in Niger. Sustainability **12**, 1802 (2020). https://doi.org/10.3390/su12051802

35. Passerotti, G., Massazza, G., Pezzoli, A., Bigi, V., Zsótér, E., Rosso, M.: Hydrological model application in the Sirba River: early warning system and GloFAS improvements. Water **12**, 620 (2020). https://doi.org/10.3390/w12030620

36. Massazza, G., et al.: Downscaling regional hydrological forecast for operational use in local early warning: HYPE models in the Sirba River. Water **12**, 3504 (2020). https://doi.org/10.3390/w12123504

37. Tiepolo, M., Rosso, M., Massazza, G., Belcore, E., Issa, S., Braccio, S.: Flood assessment for risk-informed planning along the Sirba River, Niger. Sustainability **11**, 4003 (2019). https://doi.org/10.3390/su11154003

38. Belcore, E., Pezzoli, A., Massazza, G., Rosso, M., Piras, M.: Raspberry Pi 3 multispectral low-cost sensor for UAV-based remote sensing. Case study in South-West Niger. Int. Arch. Photogramm. Remote Sens. Spatial Inf. Sci. **XLII-2/W13**, 207–214 (2019). https://doi.org/10.5194/isprs-archives-XLII-2-W13-207-2019

39. Cai, C., Gao, Y.: Precise point positioning using combined GPS and GLONASS observations. J. GPS **6**, 13–22 (2007). https://doi.org/10.5081/jgps.6.1.13

40. Dawidowicz, K., Krzan, G.: Coordinate estimation accuracy of static precise point positioning using on-line PPP service, a case study. Acta Geod. Geophys. **49**, 37–55 (2014). https://doi.org/10.1007/s40328-013-0038-0

41. Dabove, P., Piras, M., Jonah, K.N.: Statistical comparison of PPP solution obtained by online post-processing services. In: 2016 IEEE/ION Position, Location and Navigation Symposium (PLANS) (2016)

42. Mireault, Y., Tétreault, P., Lahaye, F., Héroux, P., Kouba, J.: Online precise point positioning: a new, timely service from natural resources Canada. GPS World **19**, 59–64 (2008)

43. Natural Resources Canada Natural Resources Canada. https://webapp.geod.nrcan.gc.ca/geod/tools-outils/ppp.php. Accessed 4 Sept 2019

44. Griffiths, J., Ray, J.R.: On the precision and accuracy of IGS orbits. J. Geod. **83**, 277–287 (2009). https://doi.org/10.1007/s00190-008-0237-6

45. APPS Automatic Precise Positioning Service – APPS. http://apps.gdgps.net/index.php. Accessed 4 Sept 2019

46. AUSPOS, A.G. AUSPOS - Online GPS Processing Service. https://www.ga.gov.au/scientific-topics/positioning-navigation/geodesy/auspos. Accessed 4 Sept 2019

47. Takasu, T., Yasuda, A.: Development of the low-cost RTK-GPS receiver with an open source program package RTKLIB. In: International Symposium on GPS/GNSS 2009, 1, 6

48. Choy, S., Bisnath, S., Rizos, C.: Uncovering common misconceptions in GNSS precise point positioning and its future prospect. GPS Solut. **21**, 13–22 (2017). https://doi.org/10.1007/s10291-016-0545-x

49. Seepersad, G., Bisnath, S.: Challenges in assessing PPP performance. J. Appl. Geodesy **8**, 205–222 (2014). https://doi.org/10.1515/jag-2014-0008

50. Choi, B.-K., Roh, K.-M., Lee, S.J.: Long baseline GPS RTK with estimating tropospheric delays. J. Position. Navig. Timing **3**, 123–129 (2014). https://doi.org/10.11003/JPNT.2014.3.3.123

51. NovAtel Resolving Errors. https://www.novatel.com/an-introduction-to-gnss/chapter-5-resolving-errors/. Accessed 12 Nov 2019

52. Li, P., Zhang, X.: Integrating GPS and GLONASS to accelerate convergence and initialisation times of precise point positioning. GPS Solut **18**, 461–471 (2014). https://doi.org/10.1007/s10291-013-0345-5

53. Ren, X., Choy, S., Harima, K., Zhang, X.: Multi-Constellation GNSS precise point positioning using GPS, GLONASS and BeiDou in Australia. In: International Global Navigation Satellite Systems Society, pp. 1–13 (2015)

The Use of Volunteered Geographic Information to Explore Informal Trail Networks in Protected Areas

Luís Monteiro[1]([✉]) [iD] and Pedro Cabral[1,2] [iD]

[1] NOVA Information Management School (NOVA IMS), Universidade Nova de Lisboa, Campus de Campolide, 1070-312 Lisboa, Portugal
g20210017@novaims.unl.pt
[2] School of Remote Sensing and Geomatics Engineering, Nanjing University of Information Science and Technology, Nanjing 210044, China

Abstract. Volunteered Geographic Information is a form of user-generated content, organized in applications and online platforms which compile information about recreational uses. These data are mostly freely available and seen as alternatives to trail inventories and visitor surveys. VGI is useful in studies on informal trail networks to assess visitor-related impacts which may disturb natural and cultural conditions, affecting local resources and causing landscape fragmentation through large scale processes. The present research explores the use of georeferenced tracks from an outdoor sports website, as an alternative resource to assess the distribution of informal trails, their spatial and temporal use, and related impacts in the Arrábida Nature Park, Portugal. A total of 2495 individual tracks, of the 3923 tracks initially downloaded (28911,254 km) were passing through the study area, with 2100 using the official roads and marked trails, while 395 were using the informal trail network. Hiking and biking are the activities that most use informal trails and the places with the highest intensity of use are located between Vale da Rasca and Aldeia Grande. As for landscape fragmentation, there is a decrease in all management zones, with more than 90% of the change in higher protection areas. The proposed method allowed the provision of important insights regarding how the territory is being used, making it also a valuable and alternative resource to assess the spatial distribution of informal trail networks in protected areas and assess the related fragmentation effects.

Keywords: Informal trails · Volunteered geographic information · Outdoor activities · Protected areas

1 Introduction

In 2017, the United Nations declared the International Year of Sustainable Tourism for Development, partially to address the growth of "overtourism" and its negative consequences, as predictions stated a steady growth of visitors through the coming decade [1, 2]. The world protected areas did not escape the general concerns, as they represent an

C. Grueau et al. (Eds.): GISTAM 2021/2022, CCIS 1908, pp. 86–101, 2023.
https://doi.org/10.1007/978-3-031-44112-7_6

important destination for nature-based tourism, outdoor recreation, and leisure activities, with over eight billion visits to terrestrial designated sites every year [3]. Recent changes in the global society, such as the democratization of global traveling, technological advances, and social media, and new trends regarding healthier lifestyles, including the practice of regular physical exercise are pointed out as the reasons for this upward trend [4].

Recently, the COVID-19 pandemic has disrupted general visitation trends due to travel restrictions, and many consequences reached far beyond the health implications, challenging protected areas worldwide [5]. Despite that, in the urban context, the outbreak demonstrated the importance of nature for city residents, when relaxation opportunities are limited, with urban natural and protected areas experiencing considerable levels of visitation [6, 7]. In some cases, parks and particularly paths and trails had to be closed to prevent virus transmission due to overcrowding, but also to avoid visitor-related impacts due to non-compliance with site rules [8].

The uptick in visitation has the potential to create a two-sided negative impact - a decline in the quality of recreational opportunities the sites are expected to provide; and related impacts on the ecosystem components, local communities, and infrastructure of these places [9]. Thus, in order to achieve the necessary balance between conserving biodiversity and providing compatible visitor experiences, park managers must recognize that both sides must be managed equally to properly protect these areas [10, 11]. This is the case of recreational trails, an important infrastructure present in many protected areas, that is used as a common strategy to minimize impacts by concentrating visitor flow on appropriate trail surfaces [12, 13].

When formal trail networks fail to provide the desired access, and movement within natural areas, users often tend to widen paths or venture off-trail, leading to the appearance of new informal trails, created casually or deliberately by foot trampling or bike traffic [14, 15]. Both networks of formal and informal trails can create a range of direct and indirect impacts on vegetation, wildlife, hydrology, and soils [16–19], although as informal trails are generally poorly located, lacking proper design, construction, and maintenance, there are greater impacts reported on these networks [12, 13]. Trail use can damage sensitive vegetation, due to trampling, leading to a decline in plant communities extension, height, and composition [16, 20–23]. Trampling can also result in soil erosion and compaction, with further effects on soil loss, nutrient leaching, and soil microbiology [16, 24–31]. Impacts can also include the introduction and spread of invasive species and pathogens, and as well displacement of wildlife [32–37]. At the landscape scale, trail networks may also exacerbate ecological fragmentation effects in relatively undisturbed habitats, by reducing plant communities, altering environmental conditions of vegetation patches, and restraining the movement of species [38–41].

Landscape fragmentation effects of formal infrastructures, such as roads and trails, have long been a concern among land managers and researchers [32, 33, 44, 45], contrasting with limited studies on landscape level impacts related to informal trail networks [19, 46]. As informal trails are composed of several short segments with complex patterns, assessing their extended impacts is considering the main challenge when implementing extensive monitoring campaigns in protected areas [47–49]. This is particularly important for many protected areas, in particular, those with limited resources, as common informal trail inventories, are time and resources demanding, as they are performed using hand-held GPS units and walking through the entire network system [12].

There has been a considerable increase in the number of people consuming, creating, and sharing their recreational and leisure experiences on social media platforms, which presents an endless opportunity to acquire information over large areas in a time and cost-free way [50, 51]. As such, a growing focus on new methods and sources of data for assessing spatial and temporal patterns of visitors' use is now rising, including interest in user-generated content from social media and geographic content provided voluntarily by people (VGI) [52, 53]. Such data had been used to estimate global nature-based recreation [54], identify spatial patterns in park popularity [55], assess spatial patterns, estimate the attractiveness of outdoor and adventure offers [56], identify popular locations, and estimate the volume of visitor flows [57], and to measure use intensity and places of potential conflict of uses [58]. Beyond the physical aspect, recreational activities have become also a motive for social networking, with dedicated fitness and travel websites and mobile phone applications compiling VGI data in a variety of formats. Among them, georeferenced tracks of users' routes are a common component of VGI, that are recorded with GPS-enabled devices or created with specific software, together with secondary specific information (e.g., user data, type of activity, level of difficulty, points of interest, etc.), representing recreational activities that are usually developed along roads and trail networks. As they are composed of multiple points with geotag data (i.e., lat/long coordinates), and information on the altitude and distance, they can provide useful information regarding the type of user and activity, and related spatial and temporal behavior of people in recreational and protected area trails.

As more VGI of recreational activities are freely available to the public on the internet, without apparent control over what is uploaded, users are motivated to explore new routes and destinations, regardless of the rules and regulations in place. Therefore, GPS tracks will naturally reflect the spatial distribution of use in informal trails, by comparing it with the existent formal infrastructures, making it possible to make an approximation of the extent of the informal trail network within a recreational area in an effective, cheap, and accurate way [59].

This research extends the study by Monteiro and Cabral [60], by also exploring the use of GPS tracks from an outdoor sports platform for mapping and assessing informal trail networks in protected areas. Nevertheless, the present study intended to go deeper by showing the potential of VGI to assess the temporal patterns of recreational use along the PNAr infrastructures; the intensity of use along informal trail networks; and the amount of change in the PNAr management zones, as a result of fragmentation effects from informal trails.

2 Study Site

The Arrábida Nature Park (PNAr), is a protected area with approximately 17500 ha, from which 5200 are marine reserve, located in the municipalities of Sesimbra, Palmela, and Setúbal, 35 km south of Lisbon (Fig. 1). The PNAr is an important natural area located within the Lisbon Metropolitan Area (near 2,8 million inhabitants), which attracts many tourists and local visitors from the region, due to its high-quality landscapes and privilege location in the Metropolitan Area.

The rich ecosystems of the PNAr, which are created by a combination of its geology, vegetation, and location, are home to numerous rare, threatened and endangered species of fauna and flora that are included in the Natura 2000 Network. For the park management, it established four main management zones: Urban, Complementary Protection, Partial Protection, and Total Protection.

Most of the PNAr activities are performed using the local trail system network, but although there is a high demand for outdoor recreation within the park, there is a limited offer regarding formal recreational infrastructures for activities such as hiking and cycling. The formal trail system network's total length is 82,9 km and includes eleven designated trails.

The PNAr is facing growing pressure from being densely populated, and increasing demand for outdoor activities, primarily on weekends, notorious effects of park visitation can be observed along trails, with impacts such as root exposure, soil erosion, and an extensive informal trail network. As a result, informal trail development leads to an unregulated influx of tourists and visitors to more sensitive areas within the park, making their assessment and related impacts a challenging task for park managers.

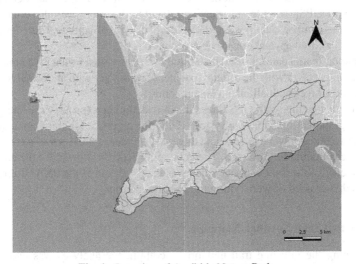

Fig. 1. Location of Arrábida Nature Park.

3 Material and Methods

This study assessed the informal trail-related fragmentation impacts from recreational activities within the PNAr using recreational volunteer data collected from a crowd-sourced online platform, as a way to describe the spatial patterns of 30 recreational activities developed along trails. Cycling, hiking, and running were treated individually in further analysis, and the remaining activities were aggregated in two big groups, motorized, and others, following the mobility typology proposed by [61]. A reason for this is also, as, in other studies, these three activities are the most common activities developed on trails in the Portuguese context [56, 62]. The following section introduces the data source and method used in the study, beginning with the collection of the dataset, the data processing and spatial analysis of GPS tracks using a GIS, and the assessment of trail-based fragmentation using predefined landscape metrics.

3.1 VGI Data Collection and Processing

The main dataset used in the research was collected from the Wikiloc website [63], a popular crowdsourced online platform, that operates since 2006, for storing and sharing GPS tracks of recreational activities. Wikiloc has one of the best data coverage in Europe, and it proved to be a suitable data source for assessing off-trail use in protected areas [59, 62]. By August 2022, more than 35 M tracks (850000 for Portugal) existed on the platform, shared by approximately 10 M users around the world.

GPS tracks were downloaded from Wikiloc using Setúbal, Sesimbra, and Palmela municipalities as the main search criteria, and considering all activities that are suitable to be developed in trails. As Wikiloc queries impose a download limit to a few GPS tracks per user/day, web scraping techniques were used to download the final VGI dataset. In addition to the GPS track file, information related to the tracks was also collected, such as route name/number, date posted, date recorded, type of activity, route length, route type (linear or circular), and downloads received.

Additional spatial datasets used in the study were provided by the PNAr management staff, including a layer with the official road network, a layer with all formal trails within the park, and a layer with all management zones.

All layers, together with GPS tracks downloaded in.gpx format were later imported into a Geographical Information System (GIS) for preprocessing and analysis. Duplicated tracks, routes drawn by users, and those with evident spatial errors were eliminated unless the error could be corrected. The debugging process allowed for the creation of a clean shapefile of the final dataset, which was later overlaid to the PNAr limits to select all routes that crossed or were within the park boundaries.

3.2 Informal Trail Network Mapping

For extracting the informal trail network, a compliance analyses was used to assess the GPS tracks that used the official PNAr infrastructure, composed of the park roads and formal trail network. Due to the nature of GPS data, a 30 m width buffer of the formal infrastructure was created, to minimize all positional errors due to deficient GNSS reception under inadequate atmospheric conditions and canopy cover [64]. This process allowed extracting all tracks that intersected the buffer's polygons, activities complying with the park's formal infrastructure, and those that did not (selection, dissolve, and erase functions), activities that used informal trails.

The resulting trail networks datasets were used in conjunction with PNAr data to conduct 3 analyses:

1. Comparison of formal and informal trail network extent, by summarizing and comparing the lineal extent of both infrastructures within the park limits, and across different management zones;

2. Assessment of relative use intensity along the informal trail network, using a square grid of 25 m to generate a raster map with the number of times a GPS track, that uses the informal trail network, crosses each cell. The resulting raster's cells store the different intensities of use, that were further reclassified in 6 quantiles, following Campelo and Nogueira Mendes [62];

3. Evaluation of informal trail-related fragmentation at the landscape level, adopting a method similar to Wimpey and Marion [12], were different landscape metrics (Number of Patches; Mean Patch Size; Largest Patch Index; Mean Perimeter: Area Ratio) were calculated for both networks (Table 1). The PNAr management zone layer was used to summarize and compare related fragmentation effects across different zones. This comparison emphasizes the effects of both networks and gives insight into the degree to which they have already contributed to the fragmentation of that landscape.

Table 1. Landscape fragmentation metrics.

Metric name	Description
Number of Patches	Number of patches of the corresponding patch type
Mean Patch Size (MPS)	Average patch size in a total class area (m^2)
Largest Patch Index (LPI)	Area of the largest patch of the corresponding patch type divided by total landscape area (m^2)
Perimeter-Area Ratio (PAR)	Ratio of the patch perimeter (m) to area (m^2)

4 Results

The final dataset downloaded from Wikiloc consisted of 3923 individual tracks, representing a total accumulated of 28911,254 km, with 63,6% of the tracks (2495 tracks) crossing the limits of PNAr (Fig. 2). This subdataset was uploaded into the platform between March 2006 and October 2021, by 189 users, which contributed with 2421 tracks (97% of the total). The remaining 74 tracks were submitted by anonymous users.

Considering the temporal track upload into the Wikiloc platform, as a possible indicator of use seasonality for different activities, over the years, most categories were uploaded during the spring months of March and April, and autumn months of October and November (Fig. 3).

According to the considered search criteria, tracks of the hiking category were the most commonly uploaded than any other type of activity, with 1016 tracks submitted by 91 different users, and "others" activities were the less uploaded category within the dataset (Table 3).

4.1 Comparison of Formal and Informal Trail Network Extent

As for the lineal extent of use on each network, a total of 3839,414 km of tracks were considered using the PNAr formal infrastructure, and the remaining 669,586 km used the informal trail network (Table 2).

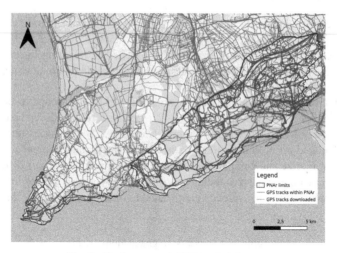

Fig. 2. Study area and GPS tracks' dataset.

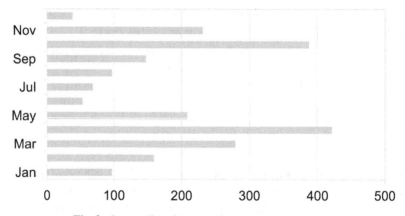

Fig. 3. Seasonality of GPS tracks present in the dataset.

Table 2. Linear extent of GPS tracks using the PNAr formal infrastructure and informal trail network.

Track type	Number of tracks	Km	Km/track
Formal infrastructure	2100	3839,945	1,829
Informal trail network	395	669,603	1,695

When considering the linear extent of formal and informal networks through the PNAr management zones, 66% of the informal trail network appears in the complementary protection zone, 27% in partial protection, and the remaining 7% in full protection. These results represent potential management conflicts between current uses and each management zone.

Table 3. Number of GPS tracks and related lineal extent of each activity along the PNAr formal infrastructure and informal trail network.

Activity	On formal infrastrcture		On informal trails	
	N tracks	Km	N tracks	Km
Cycling	528 (21,2%)	96547,189	107 (4,3%)	181,385
Hiking	877 (35,2%)	160363,417	159 (6,4%)	269,535
Running	345 (13,8%)	63084,811	86 (3,4%)	145,786
Motorized	261 (10,5%)	47725,031	32 (1,3%)	54,246
Others	89 (3,6%)	16274,053	11 (0,4%)	18,647

4.2 Assessment of Relative Use Intensity Along the Informal Trail Network

When using a map algebra approach to analyse the use intensity on the formal infrastructure of the Park and informal trail network, results from the raster calculator show that 31,19% of the cells were present along the formal infrastructure, and 40420 were cells with use just on informal trails (Table 4).

Table 4. Summary of use intensity assessment along the PNAr formal infrastructure and informal trail network.

Track type	Number of cells	%
Formal infrastructure	62573	31,19
Informal trail network	40420	20,15

As for the intensity of use on informal trails, considering the reclassification of the dataset in a 6 quantile, over 26% of cells are present between Q1, with low levels of use, and on the other side 6648 of cells are in Q6, corresponding to high levels of use. These high levels of use are mainly located between the villages of Vale da Rasca and Aldeia Grande, but also close to Cabo Espichel and along the Serra do Louro (Fig. 4).

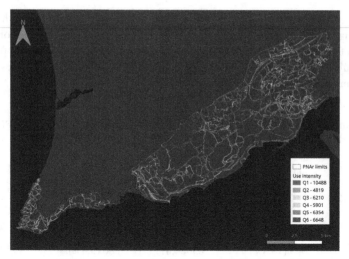

Fig. 4. Use intensity along the informal trail network.

4.3 Assessment of Informal Trail-Related Fragmentation at the Landscape Level

Fragmentation metrics results were generated for formal infrastructure and informal trails, and comparisons were done plotting them against the PNAr management zonation plan. The results of the fragmentation analysis applied at each management zone are shown in Table 5.

Every management zone experienced a substantial increase in the number of patches when including the informal trail network in the metric analysis, with the Partial P. Zone presenting the biggest increase in the number of patches (+427,6%). As for the Mean Patch Size, on the other hand, there was a decrease in all management zones for this metric between both networks. The Total P. Zone was particularly affected, presenting the biggest numeric decrease in MPS (84006,13 m²). In part because infrastructural, such as roads and trails, development in this management zone is relatively absent, making informal trails the main drivers of fragmentation.

A comparison of results of the Largest Patch metric for the formal infrastructure and the analysis including the informal trail network showed an increase for the Partial P. and Total P. Zones, while for the other management zones the Index decreased. The Mean Perimeter Ratio comprised an increase for all zones, but the Urban Zone has experienced the biggest proportional effect, increasing 126,7%

Regarding the percentage of change between the fragmentation with formal infrastructure and informal trail network, all management zones experienced a major overall decline in their area, with the Total Protection zones, suffering a decline of more than 90% with the effects of informal trails (Fig. 5).

Table 5. Landscape fragmentation indices across the PNAr management zones, and percentage of change.

	Managem. zones	Area (ha)	NP	MPS	LIP	MPR
Formal infrastructure	Urban	224,90	478	8816,63	0,87	0,04
	Complementary P.	4033,00	388	48205,55	6,55	0,02
	Partial P	4664,12	29	124709,85	3,33	0,01
	Total P.	178,84	5	178839,41	0,71	0,01
Informal trail network	Urban	180,62	474	2881,53	0,15	0,09
	Complementary P.	3236,24	751	43092,12	6,26	0,02
	Partial P	3888,71	153	51573,67	4,67	0,02
	Total P.	161,03	11	94730,27	1,03	0,01
Percentage of change	Urban	-80,30	-0,84	-67,32	-82,76	125,00
	Complementary P	-80,24	93,56	-10,61	-4,43	0,00
	Partial P	-83,38	427,59	-58,65	40,24	100,00
	Total P.	-90,04	120,00	-47,03	45,07	0,00

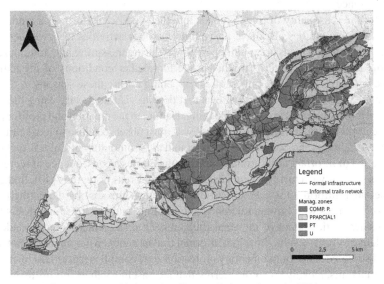

Fig. 5. Formal infrastructure and informal trail network throughout the PNAr management zones.

5   Discussion

In protected areas, commonly, informal trail studies are performed using direct methods, where extensive fieldwork is carried out, with the help of hand-held GPS units and by walking the entire network system [9]. For the present study, an alternative method is presented for mapping and assessing the impact of informal trails in the PNAr, using VGI data of recreational activities from a sport and travel dedicated platform.

The approach goes in line with recent developments in the field of visitor monitoring, where researchers and local managers are looking at VGI components as alternative sources of information to understand the spatial and temporal patterns of recreational use [65]. Approaches based on VGI are believed to produce valid preliminary results, with fewer resources needed, that can further sustain and validate management decisions in protected areas [66].

Through the years, several authors have used Wikiloc datasets to evaluate different aspects of visitor use within recreational and protected areas, such as use intensity, social conflicts, and visit and visitor characteristics [58, 61]. On the other hand, research on off-trail use using VGI data is mainly limited to sub-goals of main visitor monitoring studies. Nevertheless, the selection of Wikiloc proved to answer the main study goals, by producing a significant amount of information regarding the recreational use within the PNAr, and more specifically on informal trails and related impacts.

The number of GPS tracks existent in the final dataset (3635 tracks), could provide indications regarding the popularity of the PNAr within the Lisbon Metropolitan Area for nature-based tourism and outdoor sports could be inferred, as in other studies [56]. Although to support this conclusion, future analysis of the attractiveness of these protected areas would be required, considering visitor characteristics, such as origin, and visit preferences.

As for the seasonality of track uploads into the Wikiloc platform as an indicator of visitor use, other studies also have proved that outdoor activities in Portuguese recreational and protected areas are mainly performed during the spring and autumn seasons [56, 66]. These yearly patterns might be due to weather conditions of the temperate regions, with favorable mild temperatures happening during these seasons.

The use of the PNAr networks shows that despite visitors mostly using the official roads and trails, off-trail use is still happening, leading to the creation and proliferation of visitor-created informal trails. Informal use was most observed close to local cities, such as Azeitão, Palmela, and Setúbal, and also around the promontory of Cabo Espichel. The proliferation of informal trails around cities is many times a consequence of recreational activities generally occurring around users' residence areas or regions [40]. In the Cabo Espichel area, informal use can lead to environmental impacts, by damaging existing plant communities with limited tolerance to trampling, and soil erosion impacts [19].

Considering the extent of informal trails in each management zone to understand their relative impact, results show that informal trail use and development are not always evenly distributed. The complementary protection zone compiles the highest linear extent of informal trails, a likely fact, considering that the baseline values for this management zone already accounted for human development other than roads and trails. The presence of informal trails in the full protection zone, also shown by [67], represents management conflict as these are areas where use is forbidden due to it's high ecological value.

When comparing fragmentation at the landscape scale, it shows that fragmentation results are similar to those presented in several studies [21, 40]. In every fragmentation index, the management zones experienced substantial declines caused by the inclusion of informal trails. These are important findings, as fragmentation metrics can be used as comparative measures for the relative impacts related to the development of informal trails. Additional analysis should examine the correlation between the degrees of habitat fragmentation and the health of ecosystems, as fragmentation can cause edge effects, producing impacts on the functional and structural components of the vegetation [68, 69].

6 Conclusion

During the COVID-19 pandemic, people in Metropolitan Areas have actively sought time outside for restorative and wellness benefits. Given the extraordinary numbers of people turning to outdoor recreation in these times, potential impacts can appear in local recreational and protected areas, leading to a decrease in the quality of the visitors' experience.

The development and proliferation of informal trails is one of these impacts, that can compromise the conservation value objectives of many urban and peri-urban protected areas. As such, this research is the first to apply a VGI-based approach to assess the extent of informal trails and related impact effects at a landscape scale. It develops on the limited research field of informal trail impacts in protected areas, by developing an objective methodology, based on VGI georeferenced tracks, stored in online platforms, as an alternative solution to common extensive fieldwork.

The present study provides a snapshot of the current state of recreational use and related fragmentation impacts. Most importantly, the proposed method will allow others to update the analysis as new datasets and information are available over time. The approach intends also to stimulate further investigation and complement other monitoring techniques, such as on-site trail counters, visitor surveys, and trail conditions assessments. This will allow recreational and protected area managers to produce sustained planning decisions, by providing them with the necessary knowledge on the use of formal and informal infrastructure and allowing them to balance the needs of conservation and recreation as best as possible.

Acknowledgements. This study was partially supported through the FCT (Fundação para a Ciência e a Tecnologia) under the projects PTDC/CTA-AMB/28438/2017—ASEBIO and UIDB/04152/2020—Centro de Investigação em Gestão de Informação (MagIC).

References

1. Atzori, R.: Destination stakeholders' perceptions of overtourism impacts, causes, and responses: the case of Big Sur, California. J. Destin. Mark. Manag. **17**, 100440 (2020)
2. Mandić, A., Petrí, L.: Governance and Management of Protected Natural Areas in the Era of Overtourism, 1st edn. Springer, Cham (2021)
3. Balmford, A R., et al.: Walk on the wild side: estimating the global magnitude of visits to protected areas. PLoS Biol **13**, e1002074 (2015)
4. Brown, G., Schebella, M.F., Weber, D.: Using participatory GIS to measure physical activity and urban park benefits. Landsc. Urban Plan. **121**, 34–44 (2014)

5. Spenceley, A., et al.: Tourism in protected and conserved areas amid the COVID-19 pandemic. Parks **27**, 103–118 (2021)

6. Jackson, S.B, Stevenson, K.T., Larson, L.R, Peterson. M., Seekamp, E.: Outdoor activity participation improves adolescents' mental health and well-being during the COVID-19 pandemic. Int. J. Environ. Res. Public Health **18**(5), 2506 (2021)

7. Volenec, Z., Abraham, J., Becker, A., Dobson, A.: Public parks and the pandemic: how park usage has been affected by COVID-19 policies. PLoS ONE **16**(5), e0251799 (2021)

8. Primack, R., Terry, C.: New social trails made during the pandemic increase fragmentation of an urban protected area. Biol. Conserv. **255**, 108993 (2021)

9. Leung, Y.-F., Marion, J.: Recreation impacts and management in wilderness: a state-of-knowledge review. In: Cole, D., McCool, S., Freimund, W., Borrie, W., O'Loughlin, J. (eds.) Wilderness science in a time of change conference, vol. 5, pp. 23–48. USDA Forest Service, Rocky Mountain Research Station, Ogden, UT, USA (2020)

10. Walden-Schreiner, C., Leung, Y.-F., Kuhn, T., Newburger, T., Tsai, W.-L.: Environmental and managerial factors associated with pack stock distribution in high elevation meadows: case study from Yosemite National Park. J. Environ. Manage. **193**, 52–63 (2017)

11. Barros, C., Moya-Gómez, B., García-Palomares, J.: Identifying temporal patterns of visitors to national parks through geotagged photographs. Sustainability **11**(24), 6983 (2019)

12. Wimpey, J., Marion, J.: A spatial exploration of informal trail networks within Great Falls Park, VA. J. Environ. Manage. **92**(3), 1012–1022 (2011)

13. Marion, J., Leung, Y.-F.: Indicators and protocols for monitoring impacts of formal and informal trails in protected areas. J. Tour. Leisure Stud. **17**(2), 215–236 (2011)

14. Wimpey, J., Marion, J.: The influence of use, environmental and managerial factors on the width of recreational trails. J. Environ. Manage. **91**, 2028–2037 (2010)

15. Havlick, D., Billmeyer, E., Huber, T., Vogt, B., Rodman, K.: Informal trail creation: hiking, trail running, and mountain bicycling in shortgrass prairie. J. Sustain. Tour. **24**(7), 1041–1058 (2015)

16. Liddle, M.: Recreation Ecology, 2nd edn. Chapman and Hall Publishing, London (1997)

17. Pickering, C., Hill, W.: Impacts of recreation and tourism on plant biodiversity and vegetation in protected areas in Australia. J. Environ. Manage. **85**(4), 791–800 (2007)

18. Newsome, D., Moore, S., Dowling, D.: Natural Area Tourism: Ecology, Impacts and Management, 2nd edn. Channel View Publishing, Bristol (2013)

19. Ballantyne, M., Pickering, C.: Differences in the impacts of formal and informal recreational trails on urban forest loss and tree structure. J. Environ. Manage. **159**, 94–105 (2015)

20. Hill, W., Pickering, C.: Vegetation associated with different walking track types in the Kosciuszko alpine area, Australia. J. Environ. Manage. **78**(1), 24–34 (2006)

21. Leung, Y.-F., Newburger, T., Jones, M., Kuhn, B., Woiderski, B.: Developing a monitoring protocol for visitor-created informal trails in Yosemite National Park, USA. J. Environ. Manage. **47**(1), 93–106 (2011)

22. Zhang, J.T., Xiang, C.L., Li, M.: Effects of tourism and topography on vegetation diversity in the subalpine meadows of the Dongling Mountains of Beijing, China. Environ. Manage. **49**(2), 403–411 (2012)

23. Barros, A., Gonnet, J., Pickering, C.: Impacts of informal trails on vegetation and soils in the highest protected area in the Southern Hemisphere. J. Environ. Manage. **127**, 50–60 (2013)

24. Wilshire, H.G., Nakata, J.K., Shipley, S., Prestegaard, K.: Impacts of vehicles on natural terrain at seven sites in the San Francisco Bay area. Environ. Geol. **2**(5), 295–319 (1978)

25. Deluca, T., Patterson, I., Freimund, W., Cole, D.: Influence of llamas, horses, and hikers on soil erosion from established recreation trails in Western Montana, USA. J. Environ. Manage. **22**, 255–262 (1998)

26. Farrell, T., Marion, J.: Trail impacts and trail impact man- agement related to visitation at Torres del Paine National Park, Chile. Leisure (Loisir) **26**, 31–59 (2001)

27. Nepal, S., Nepal, S.: Visitor impacts on trails in the Sagar- matha (Mt. Everest) National Park, Nepal. Ambio **33**, 334–340 (2004)
28. Olive, N., Marion, J.: The influence of use-related, environmental and managerial factors on soil loss from recreational trails. J. Environ. Manage. **90**, 1483–1493 (2009)
29. Lucas-Borja, M., et al.: The effects of human trampling on the microbiological properties of soil and vegetation in mediterranean mountain areas. Land Degrad. Dev. **22**, 383–394 (2011)
30. Müllerová, J., Vítková, M., Vítek, O.: The impacts of road and walking trails upon adjacent vegetation: effects of road building materials on species composition in a nutrient poor environment. Sci. Total Environ. **409**(19), 3839–3849 (2011)
31. Tomczyk, A., White, P., Ewertowski, M.: Effects of extreme natural events on the provision of ecosystem services in a mountain environment: the importance of trail design in delivering system resilience and ecosystem service co-benefits. J. Environ. Manage. **166**, 156–167 (2016)
32. Benninger-Truax, M., Vankat, J., Schaefer, R.: Trail corridors as habitat and conduits for movement of plant species in Rocky Mountain National Park, Colorado, USA. Landscape Ecol. **6**(4), 269–278 (1992)
33. Drayton, B., Primack, R.: Plant species lost in an isolated conservation area in metropolitan Boston from 1894 to 1993. Conserv. Biol. **10**(1), 30–39 (1996)
34. Taylor, A., Knight, R.: Wildlife responses to recreation and associated visitor perceptions. Ecol. Appl. **13**(4), 951–963 (2003)
35. Dickens, S., Gerhardt, F., Collinge, S.: Recreational portage trails as corridors facilitating non-native plant invasions of the Boundary Waters Canoe Area Wilderness (USA). Conserv. Biol. **19**(5), 1653–1657 (2005)
36. Marzano, M., Dandy, N.: Recreationist behaviour in forests and the disturbance to wildlife. Biodivers. Conserv. **21**(11), 2967–2986 (2012)
37. Wolf, I., Croft, D.: Impacts of tourism hotspots on vegetation communities show a higher potential for self-propagation along roads than hiking trails. J. Environ. Manage. **143**, 173–185 (2014)
38. Saunders, D., Hobbs, R., Margules, C.: Biological consequences of ecosystem fragmentation: a review. Conserv. Biol. **5**(1), 18–32 (1991)
39. Geneletti, D.: Using spatial indicators and value functions to assess ecosystem fragmentation caused by linear infrastructures. Int. J. Appl. Earth Obs. Geoinf. **5**(1), 1–15 (2004)
40. Ballantyne, M., Gudes, O., Pickering, C.: Recreational trails are an important cause of fragmentation in endangered urban forests: a case-study from Australia. Landsc. Urban Plan. **130**(1), 112–124 (2014)
41. Fahrig, L.: Ecological responses to habitat fragmentation per se. Annu. Rev. Ecol. Evol. Syst. **48**, 1–23 (2017)
42. Ripple, W., Bradshaw, G., Spies, T.: Measuring forest landscape patterns in the cascade range of Oregon, USA. Biol. Cons. **57**, 73–88 (1991)
43. Matlack, G.: Sociological edge effects: spatial distribution of human impact in suburban forest fragments. Environ. Manage. **17**(6), 829–835 (1993)
44. Swenson, J.J., Franklin, J.: The effects of future urban development on habitat fragmentation in the Santa Monica mountains. Landscape Ecol. **15**, 713–730 (2000)
45. Carsjens, G., van Lier, H.: Fragmentation and land-use planning-an introduction. Landsc. Urban Plan. **58**(2–4), 79–82 (2002)
46. Leung, Y.-F., Newburger, T., Jones, M., Kuhn. B., Woiderski, B.: Developing a monitoring protocol for visitor-created informal trails in Yosemite National Park, USA. Environ. Manage. **47**(1), 93–106 (2011)
47. Leung, Y.F., Marion, J.: Characterizing backcountry camping impacts in Great Smoky Mountains national park, USA. J. Environ. Manage. **57**(3), 193–203 (1999)

48. Monz, C., Marion, J., Goonan, K., Manning, R., Wimpey, J., Carr, C.: Assessment and monitoring of recreation impacts and resource conditions on mountain summits. Mt. Res. Dev. **30**(4), 332–343 (2010)
49. Barros, A., Pickering, C.: How networks of informal trails cause landscape level damage to vegetation. Environ. Manage. **60**(1), 57–68 (2017)
50. Wang, D., Xiang, Z., Fesenmaier, D.: Adapting to the mobile world: a model of smartphone use. Ann. Tour. Res. **48**, 11–26 (2014)
51. Dickinson, J., Hibbert, J., Filimonau, V.: Mobile technology and the tourist experience: (Dis)connection at the campsite. Tour. Manage. **57**, 193–201 (2016)
52. Heikinheimo, V., Minin, E., Tenkanen, H., Hausmann, A., Erkkonen, J., Toivonen, T.: User-generated geographic information for visitor monitoring in a national park: a comparison of social media data and visitor survey. Int. J. Geo-Inf. **6**(3), 85 (2017)
53. Walden-Schreiner, C., Leung, Y.-F., Tateosian, L.: Digital footprints: incorporating crowd sourced geographic information for protected area management. Appl. Geogr. **90**, 44–54 (2018)
54. Wood, S., Guerry, A., Silver, J., Lacayo, M.: Using social media to quantify nature-based tourism and recreation. Sci. Rep. **3**(1), 2976 (2013)
55. Levin, N., Lechner, A., Brown, G.: An evaluation of crowdsourced information for assessing the visitation and perceived importance of protected areas. Appl. Geogr. **79**, 115–126 (2017)
56. Santos, T., Nogueira Mendes, R., Farías-Torbidoni, E., Julião, R.: Volunteered geographical information and recreational uses within metropolitan and rural contexts. ISPRS Int. J. Geo Inf. **11**(2), 144 (2022)
57. Orsi, F., Geneletti, D.: Using geotagged photographs and GIS analysis to estimate visitor flows in natural areas. J. Nature Conserv. **21**, 359–368 (2013)
58. Santos, T., Nogueira Mendes, R., Vasco, A.: Recreational activities in urban parks: spatial interactions among users. J. Outdoor Recreat. Tour. **15**, 1–9 (2016)
59. Norman, P., Pickering, C.: Using volunteered geographic information to assess park visitation: comparing three on-line platforms. Appl. Geogr. **89**, 163–172 (2017)
60. Monteiro, L., Cabral, P.: Assessing informal trails impacts and fragmentation effects on protected areas using volunteered geographic information. In: Grueau, C., Ragia, L. (eds.) Proceedings of the 8th International Conference on Geographical Information Systems Theory, Applications and Management, GISTAM 2022, vol. 1, pp. 48–55 (2022)
61. Callau, A., Perez, Y., Giné, D.: Quality of GNSS traces from VGI: a data cleaning method based on activity type and user experience. Int. J. Geo-Inf. **9**(12), 727 (2010)
62. Campelo, M., Nogueira Mendes, R.: Comparing webshare services to assess mountain bike use in protected areas. J. Outdoor Recreat. Tour. **15**, 82–88 (2016)
63. Wikiloc Homepage. https://www.wikiloc.com/. Accessed 07 Oct 2021
64. Korpilo, S., Virtanen, T., Lehvävirta, S.: Smartphone GPS tracking—inexpensive and efficient data collection on recreational movement. Landsc. Urban Plan. **157**, 608–617 (2017)
65. Teles da Mota, V., Pickering, C.: Using social media to assess nature-based tourism: current research and future trends. J. Outdoor Recreat. Tour. **30**, 100295 (2020)
66. Nogueira Mendes, R., Silva, A., Grilo, C., Rosalino, L., Silva, C.: MTB monitoring in Arrábida Natural Park, Portugal. In: Fredman, P., Stenseke, M., Liljendahl, H., Mossing, A., Laveet, D. (eds.) Proceedings of the 6th International Conference on Monitoring and Management of Visitors in Recreational and Protected Areas: Outdoor Recreation in Change Current Knowledge and Future Challenges, Stockholm, Sweden, pp. 32–33 (2012)
67. Manning, R., Leung, Y.-F., Budruk, M.: Research to support management of visitor carrying capacity on Boston Harbour Islands. Northeast. Nat. **12**(3), 201–220 (2015)

68. Harper, K., MacDonald, S.: Structure and composition of edges next to regenerating clear-cuts in mixed-wood boreal forest. J. Veg. Sci. **13**(4), 535–546 (2002)
69. Moxham, C., Turner, V.: The effect of fragmentation on the threatened plant community Coastal Moonah Woodland in Victoria, Australia. Urban Ecosyst. **14**(4), 569–583 (2011)

Solar Energy Assessment: From Rooftop Extraction to Identifying Utilizable Areas

Mohammad Aslani[1(✉)] and Stefan Seipel[1,2]

[1] Department of Computer and Geo-spatial Sciences, University of Gävle, Gävle, Sweden
{Mohammad.Aslani,Stefan.Seipel}@hig.se
[2] Division of Visual Information and Interaction, Department of Information Technology, Uppsala University, Uppsala, Sweden

Abstract. Rooftop photovoltaics have been acknowledged as a critical component in cities' efforts to reduce their reliance on fossil fuels and move towards energy sustainability. Identifying rooftop areas suitable for installing rooftop photovoltaics-referred to as utilizable areas-is essential for effective energy planning and developing policies related to renewable energies. Utilizable areas are greatly affected by the size, shape, superstructures of rooftops, and shadow effects. This study estimates utilizable areas and solar energy potential of rooftops by considering the mentioned factors. First, rooftops are extracted from LiDAR data by training PointNet++, a neural network architecture for processing 3D point clouds. The second step involves extracting planar segments of rooftops using a combination of clustering and region growing. Finally, utilizable areas of planar segments are identified by removing areas that do not have a suitable size and do not receive sufficient solar irradiation. Additionally, in this step, areas reserved for accessibility to photovoltaics are removed. According to the experimental results, the methods have a high success rate in rooftop extraction, plane segmentation, and, consequently, estimating utilizable areas for photovoltaics.

Keywords: Rooftop solar energy · Spatial analyses · Plane segmentation · Rooftop extraction · Deep learning

1 Introduction

Rooftop photovoltaics have emerged as a promising solution for satisfying a portion of the energy demand in urban areas owing to their great potential for scalability and lower greenhouse gas emissions. Rooftop photovoltaics allow buildings to become active power producers, reducing their reliance on external energy sources [8]. However, not all rooftop areas are utilizable for photovoltaic deployment. Utilizable rooftop areas are limited by various factors, the most important of which are the shape, orientation, and superstructures of roofs, as well as occlusion [36]. A rooftop with proper orientation and no superstructures or surrounding objects offers high solar energy potential. In contrast, a

© The Author(s), under exclusive license to Springer Nature Switzerland AG 2023
C. Grueau et al. (Eds.): GISTAM 2021/2022, CCIS 1908, pp. 102–115, 2023.
https://doi.org/10.1007/978-3-031-44112-7_7

north-facing rooftop with many superstructures surrounded by tall buildings (in the northern hemisphere) may not offer high solar energy potential. Moreover, local climate conditions and geographical location may affect the solar energy potential of rooftops.

Manual identification of utilizable rooftop areas based on the mentioned factors can be time-consuming and even unfeasible, especially for large regions. Hence, more efficient and automated approaches are necessary to expedite the process of identifying utilizable areas. In this context, analyzing LiDAR datasets has been recognized as a potential way to automate this process [15]. LiDAR datasets provide 3D spatial profiles of the area and allow for automatic computation of characteristics of rooftops and their surrounding objects, such as area, height, tilt, and azimuth. The issue of identifying utilizable rooftop areas for photovoltaics installation has been addressed through developing spatially-based methods utilizing geoinformatics. These methods start by outlining the borders of rooftops, modeling their shapes, and identifying areas that are utilizable for rooftop photovoltaics [2,5]. These methods typically take into account the tilt, orientation, and superstructures of rooftops when identifying utilizable areas. In this study, utilizable areas of rooftops are identified using a new spatially-based method.

2   Related Work

2.1   Extraction of Rooftops and Modeling Their Form

Identifying utilizable rooftop areas entails several steps, the first of which is determining the *extent* of rooftops. This step is crucial as it provides information on the overall surface area of rooftops, which can then be used in further analyses to pinpoint utilizable areas. With the fast advancement of remote sensing technologies, point clouds of varying resolutions have become more and more accessible. Consequently, research within the field of automatic building extraction from point clouds has received widespread attention, and many methods have been developed. In these methods, points belonging to rooftops are extracted based on their geometric and morphological features that are different from other objects, such as trees and roads. In this context, a variety of machine-learning approaches have been applied.

In [21], the AdaBoost algorithm was used to classify LiDAR data into four categories: roads, grass, buildings, and trees. Different features, such as height, height variation, and normal vector variation, were used for the classification. Their method was tested on ten regions, and the evaluation results indicated an accuracy of 92%. In [3], support vector machines (SVMs) were employed to identify rooftops. They proposed a new method named data reduction based on locality-sensitive hashing (DRLSH) to automatically select training samples for SVMs. The method was evaluated on a test site in Gothenburg, Sweden, and the results showed its suitable performance. In another study [4], a different instance selection method for SVMs was developed. The method-named border point extraction based on locality-sensitive hashing (BPLSH)- was tested on several datasets, and the results showed its superiority over other methods. In [33], PointNet++ was used to identify rooftops from LiDAR datasets. It is a deep neural network architecture for 3D point cloud analysis [27]. The authors could accurately identify rooftops in point clouds, showing the potential of this deep learning architecture for 3D data analysis.

Rooftop extraction is required for different spatial applications, but reliable spatial analyses of rooftops require modeling their *shape*. This is particularly important in identifying utilizable areas as the solar suitability of rooftops and the efficiency of photovoltaics rely on rooftops' form. The angle at which a rooftop faces the sun affects the amount of sunlight that photovoltaics receives [40]. Model-driven and data-driven are two commonly used approaches for roof shape modeling.

In the model-driven approach, the rooftop shape is determined based on a predefined library of roof shapes [41]. Indeed, the approach defines a library of roof shapes and chooses a shape that best matches the point cloud or surface model. In [20], this approach was used to model the shape of rooftops in Uppsala. It ensures regularized planar patches and low sensitivity to noise as it incorporates prior knowledge about roof shapes into the modeling process. However, the performance of this approach depends on the defined library's completeness. If the library is not comprehensive enough, it may not accurately represent the rooftop shapes. Moreover, this approach may overlook rooftop superstructures (e.g., chimneys), which play an important role in identifying utilizable areas.

In the data-driven approach, planar segments are derived independently of the overall roof shape [10]. This can be quite beneficial in adhering planar segments to their underlying surface. Furthermore, this approach is not limited to a set of predetermined shapes, and thus it is capable of extracting all planar segments of any arbitrary polyhedral rooftops-including rooftop superstructures [7,16]. Various techniques are commonly utilized in the data-driven approach, such as region growing, random sample consensus (RANSAC), and clustering [38,39].

Region growing is a method to group close pixels with similar characteristics into larger regions or objects. Region growing begins with selecting a number of points (seed points) known to belong to a plane. Then, it iteratively adds neighboring points that meet coplanarity criteria until no more points can be added to the plane. Coplanarity criteria are typically based on measures such as point distance, normal vector difference, and curvature and are used to ensure that the added points are coplanar with the initial seed points. In [18], planar patches of rooftops were segmented using region growing to estimate rooftop solar potential. In [12], a method that replaces points with volumetric elements called voxels was presented to enhance the computational efficiency of region growing. The performance of region growing is greatly affected by how the seeds are arranged and the accuracy of the estimations of surface properties such as normal direction and curvature at various points.

In RANSAC-based methods for plane segmentation, a subset of samples is chosen each time, plane models fit each subset, and the model with the most inliers is chosen. Inliers are points that lie close to the fitted plane model, while outliers lie far away from the fitted plane model. In [10], RANSAC was used for plane segmentation. Despite the simplicity of classical RANSAC, applying it to plane segmentation in point clouds may result in the detection of spurious planes. Several variations and adaptations of RANSAC have been developed to overcome this issue [38].

Clustering-based methods form planar segments by grouping points with similar features, where the definition of features should enable clear differentiation of planar segments. In a well-defined feature space, points on the same planar segment should be mapped close together. In [31], a clustering-based plane segmentation method based on normal vectors was proposed. The segmentation process uses fuzzy k-means clustering, and a validity index-the degree of compactness and separation of the resulting clusters-is used to obtain the optimal number of clusters. Moreover, a planarity test that distinguishes planar from non-planar points is incorporated to enhance clustering. In [22], density-based spatial clustering of applications with noise (DBSCAN) [13] was used to extract planar segments of rooftops. The feature space for clustering was defined using position, slope, azimuth, and shadow. The choice of clustering algorithm is crucial in this class of methods, and clustering algorithms with high time complexity might be impractical for handling high-resolution point clouds.

2.2   Identification of Rooftop Utilizable Areas

Different factors limit utilizable areas of rooftops for installing photovoltaics [32]. Rooftop superstructures (e.g., chimneys), shadow effects caused by adjacent buildings or trees, and regulations governing the installation of photovoltaics are among the factors that impose limitations [6]. Identifying utilizable areas is critical to avoid overestimating the potential of rooftop solar energy, which could lead to unrealistic expectations and inaccurate planning for integrating solar energy into existing power infrastructures. By considering utilizable areas, developing more informed and realistic strategies for deploying photovoltaics is possible, which can contribute to the transition towards more sustainable energy systems [15,25].

The challenge of identifying utilizable areas has been the subject of numerous studies [9]. A commonly used method for identifying these areas is to use a set of loss coefficients, which indicate the average reduction in available rooftops [29]. These coefficients are determined based on simplified assumptions about rooftops, such as a proportion of rooftops mainly in shadow or used for non-photovoltaic purposes (e.g., air conditioning and accessibility). Although this approach is computationally fast, adapting coefficients to new areas is not trivial, and unsuitable loss coefficients may result in overlooking rooftop variations [35].

To address this issue, a few spatially-based methods have been recently proposed. However, most of the proposed spatially-based methods are limited to manual digitization [11] or simplified roof shape modeling [20], or they may not consider shadow effects [23]. This study identifies utilizable areas with more spatial details by analyzing roof shapes, roof superstructures, and shadow effects. It aims to automatically (a) extract rooftops using a deep learning-based method, (b) segment planar rooftop patches using a clustering-based method, and (c) identify utilizable areas using morphological operations.

3   Methods

In this section, the procedure for identifying utilizable areas and estimating the solar energy potential of rooftops is detailed. It relies on using LiDAR datasets, which can provide detailed 3D information about an area. It assumes that the LiDAR data has enough density to accurately capture the shape of the rooftops and superstructures that may affect solar energy potential estimates. The major steps of the procedure are explained in the following sections.

3.1   Extraction of Rooftops

The task of rooftop identification falls within the domain of semantic segmentation, in which the objective is to detect points that constitute rooftops. Deep learning methods have made significant progress in recent years and demonstrated impressive results in various semantic segmentation tasks, making them suitable for this purpose. Our study employs PointNet++, a state-of-the-art deep learning architecture designed to handle point cloud data such as LiDAR [27]. PointNet++ is a hierarchical neural network for semantic segmentation of unorganized point data, and it enables multiscale point feature learning. It has the potential to be trained without requiring parameters that are specific to objects in LiDAR. A PointNet++ network consists of sampling, grouping, and mini-PointNet layers. The sampling layer chooses points that form the centroids of local regions. The grouping layer constructs local region sets around the centroids. The mini-PointNet layer abstracts the sets of local features into higher-level representations using a series of convolution, normalization, relu, and max-pooling layers. Please refer to [27] for more details. To effectively train PointNet++ for rooftop extraction, we utilize labeled point cloud datasets encompassing various rooftop features. These labeled datasets provide crucial information on the structure, geometry, and spatial distribution of rooftop points, enabling the network to learn and recognize the distinguishing characteristics of rooftops.

3.2   Rooftop Plane Segmentation

This step involves dividing rooftops into planar or flat regions. It is necessary to identify utilizable areas as planar segments unobstructed by superstructures (e.g., chimneys) provide stable and consistent surfaces for mounting photovoltaics. Plane segmentation is performed on digital surface models (DSMs); thus, the recognized rooftop LiDAR point clouds are converted into DSMs. Planar segments are extracted by clustering, and the feature space for clustering is defined by normal vectors of pixels obtained by fitting a plane to the pixel and its neighbors. Pixels on the same planar segment have similar normal vectors; thus, planar patches can be identified by grouping them together. Some pixels in each planar segment may, however, have normal vectors that are inconsistent with those of other pixels in the same segment. These pixels are known as non-planar pixels, as they are placed in the vicinity of more than one plane. Including these pixels in clustering may disturb the creation of planar segments since they shatter the boundaries of clusters of normal vectors. As a result, non-planar pixels must be identified and excluded from clustering. Principle component analysis (PCA) is used to evaluate the planarity of each pixel.

To cluster normal vectors, a minimum density divisive clustering (MDDC) algorithm is used [26]. MDDC is a density-based hierarchical clustering algorithm, which assumes continuous regions of low probability density separate clusters. Clusters are formed by hyperplanes that pass through regions with low probability density. The adaptability (i.e., it requires no input parameters) and high computational efficiency of MDDC make it suitable for handling large datasets. Since segmentation using MDDC does not consider the spatial connectivity of pixels, each resulting patch may comprise multiple parallel planar segments that are spatially separated. To split multi-part patches, Euclidean clustering based on pixel coordinates is applied [30]. Finally, the non-planar pixels, initially excluded, are assigned to the best segment using region growing. In this manner, the issue of over-segmentation that could potentially occur during clustering is also addressed.

3.3 Rooftop Utilizable Areas

This stage entails calculating the solar energy potential of rooftops. Since it is not feasible to install photovoltaic panels across the entire rooftop surface, determining the utilizable areas for photovoltaics is crucial to prevent the overestimation of energy generation. Utilizable areas refer to specific rooftop sections where photovoltaic installation is practical. Therefore, every planar segment undergoes a thorough spatial analysis to pinpoint these utilizable areas.

Portions of planar segments need to remain clear of photovoltaics to maintain accessibility, which is an essential requirement for panel installation. Frequently, a gap between the photovoltaic edge and the segment, known as the service area, must be preserved. To exclude these areas, we utilize a morphological erosion operation with a circular structuring element whose radius is equal to the width of the service areas [34]. The erosion operation shrinks the roof face by the width of the service area. In addition to service areas, there might be some areas of planar segments that are too small for a photovoltaic to fit, and these areas should be excluded. To accomplish this, we use morphological opening operations in accordance with Algorithm 1. The inputs to the algorithm include a segment RF_T obtained from the previous step, a structuring element representing a solar panel SP, and a set of angles Δ for rotating the structuring element. The algorithm applies a series of opening operations with varying directions of the structuring element, as solar panels can be installed in different directions in practice. Each iteration identifies regions in the segment that can accommodate a rotated solar panel through the opening operation. The output RF_{TG} is the merging of all suitable regions obtained over the iterations.

Algorithm 1. Pseudo-code for removing areas that cannot accommodate a solar panel.

Input: A shrunken segment RF_T
      A solar panel SP with a size of RPV_{size}
      A set of rotation angles $\Delta = \{0°, 10°, 20°, \cdots, 170°\}$
Output: A segment without geometrically unsuitable parts RF_{TG}

1: $RF_{TG} \leftarrow$ a zero matrix with a size of RF_T
2: **for each** $\theta \in \Delta$ **do**
3:    $SP_\theta \leftarrow$ rotate SP with an angle of θ
4:    $I_\theta \leftarrow O_{SP_\theta}[RF_T]$ $\%O_{SP_\theta}$ is an opening operation with structuring element SP_θ

5:    $RF_{TG} \leftarrow union(RF_{TG}, I_\theta)$
6: **end for**
7: $RF_{TG}^c \leftarrow connected\ component\ labeling(RF_{TG})$
8: **for each** $RF_{TG}^r \in RF_{TG}^c$ **do**
9:   **if** $area(RF_{TG}^r) > area(SP)$ **then**
10:     Preserve RF_{TG}^r
11:   **end if**
12: **end for**

Once geometrically incompatible areas have been eliminated; the residual planar segments undergo assessment for solar irradiation. Segments with average solar irradiation falling below a designated threshold SI are excluded, as photovoltaic installations typically avoid rooftop areas with insufficient sunlight. This process helps discard segments predominantly in the shade or those with unfavorable tilts (e.g., excessively steep) or azimuths (e.g., facing north), resulting in the identification of utilizable areas for photovoltaic installation.

By having utilizable areas, the energy potential of rooftops is determined. A rooftop's total solar electricity yield is calculated according to Eq. 1. E is the total solar electricity yield of a rooftop in kWh. S_i and ψ_i are the total solar irradiance (in kWh/m^2) and the tilt angle of the i-th utilizable segment. α and β are the efficiency and performance ratio of the photovoltaics, d is the area of each pixel of the DSM (in m^2), and N is the number of utilizable segments of a rooftop.

$$E = \alpha \cdot \beta \cdot d \cdot \sum_{i=1}^{N} \frac{S_i}{\cos \psi_i} \tag{1}$$

4   Datasets, Results and Discussion

Two datasets are employed in this study to evaluate the performance of the methods. Dayton Annotated LiDAR Earth Scan (DALES) is the first dataset

[37] used to train and evaluate PointNet++ for rooftop extraction. As a publicly accessible resource, DALES offers a comprehensive assortment of LiDAR data from various environments, making it well-suited for deep network training. The dataset encompasses 40 manually labeled scenes. The second dataset encompasses an area within Uppsala city, Sweden, and its LiDAR point cloud was created by the Uppsala municipality. This dataset serves the purpose of plane segmentation and solar energy calculation. To facilitate plane segmentation assessment, we manually identified and labeled planar segments of rooftops and used them as ground truth data. Some scenes from the datasets are shown in Fig. 1.

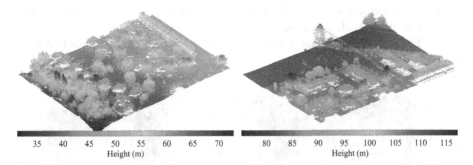

Fig. 1. Some sample scenes from the LiDAR datasets.

The results obtained by applying the procedure to the datasets are presented and discussed. The first step of the procedure is to extract rooftops, which is done by utilizing PointNet++. Of the 40 scenes in the DALES dataset, 29 are designated for training, while the rest serve as test samples. Individual scenes are subdivided into non-overlapping 50-by-50-meter tiles to maximize the dataset's utility. Each tile is then downsampled to contain only 9000 points, speeding up the training process. To train the deep network, the Adam optimizer with a gradient decay rate of 0.9 is used [19]. The maximum number of training epochs is set to 20, with each epoch consisting of 485 iterations. At the beginning of the training, the learning rate is set to 0.0005 and is reduced by a factor of 0.1 in epoch 10. Regularization is used to minimize overfitting, and the regularization factor is set to 0.1 [24].

The performance of the trained deep network for rooftop extraction is assessed by applying it to the test scenes and comparing its predictions with the ground truth labels. To quantitatively evaluate the similarity between predicted and actual labels, accuracy and intersection over union (IOU) are employed as measurement metrics. These metrics are calculated according to Eqs. 2 and 3, where TP, FP, and FN are the numbers of true positives, false positives, and false negatives, respectively.

$$Accuracy = \frac{TP}{TP + FN} \tag{2}$$

$$IOU = \frac{TP}{TP + FP + FN} \tag{3}$$

The results show that the trained deep network has an accuracy of 92.60% and an IOU of 87.38% on average in the test scenes of the DALES dataset, showing its satisfactory performance in rooftop extraction. Thus, the trained deep network can be applied to any area. We employ it in the extraction of rooftops from the second dataset. Figure 2 shows some examples of rooftop extraction from the second dataset. The boundaries of rooftops have been extracted and regularized using α-shape [1] and polyline compression [17] algorithms, respectively. The figure shows that rooftops have been effectively distinguished from other objects.

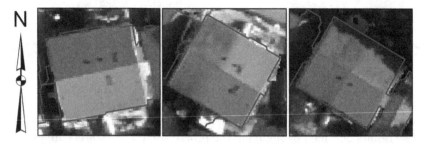

Fig. 2. Some identified rooftops. The underlying orthophoto serves solely for visualization purposes.

Subsequently, planar patches of rooftops are segmented using clustering, followed by region growing. The MDDC algorithm used for clustering normal vectors does not require prior knowledge regarding the dataset as input parameters, and it adaptively determines the shape and number of clusters in the data. The angle and height thresholds used in region growing were set to $7°$ and $10\,cm$. These values were obtained using trial and error in a small part of the dataset. Figure 3 shows plane segmentation results of some rooftops. It illustrates the effectiveness of the plane segmentation method in detecting roof faces. Small superstructures, such as vents and small chimneys, that are not identifiable as distinct planar segments appear as openings within the segments. In this way, the impact of superstructures can be considered in the identification of utilizable areas. By comparing the plane segmentation results with the ground truth data, the performance of plane segmentation is quantified in terms of accuracy and IOU. The assessment results show that the plane segmentation method has an accuracy of 98.69% and an IOU of 98.22%, suggesting that most planar segments have been accurately detected.

Fig. 3. The outcome of plane segmentation for some rooftops.

To effectively locate areas utilizable for photovoltaic deployment, a rooftop solar irradiation map is necessary, in conjunction with planar segments. This is attributed to the need for cost-efficiency, which discourages the installation of photovoltaic systems in regions with low solar irradiation. The solar irradiation of each segment is estimated using the solar model of ArcGIS Desktop [14,28]. The solar model incorporates viewshed analysis to account for shadowing effects. The viewshed analysis generates a Boolean image indicating the extent to which the sky is occluded by surrounding objects as seen from a certain place in the DSM. In addition to occlusion, the solar model takes into account site orientation, atmospheric effects, and variations in the sun's position, making it a reliable tool for estimating global solar irradiation. Figure 4 illustrates the annual global solar irradiation distribution across some rooftops, computed with ArcGIS Desktop. The impact of shadows cast by surrounding objects is evident in this figure.

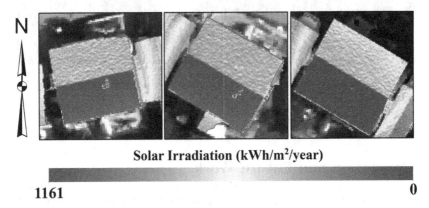

Solar Irradiation (kWh/m²/year)

1161   **0**

Fig. 4. Annual global solar irradiation of some rooftops.

Rooftop areas utilizable for solar panels are determined by excluding service areas, geometrically unsuitable areas, and areas with low solar irradiation. An erosion operation whose structuring element has a radius of 30 cm is used to remove service areas. Next, a series of opening operations are performed to discard areas incapable of accommodating photovoltaic panels. The size of the structuring elements of opening operations is set to 1.7 m × 1.0 m, which is the common size of a commercial rooftop photovoltaic panel. Moreover, the solar irradiation threshold SI used to remove low-irradiated areas is set to 1000 kWh/m^2/year. Figure 5 shows the resulting utilizable areas of some rooftops in the dataset. The figure clearly illustrates how the methodology takes into account minor superstructures, indicated by white circles, when identifying utilizable areas. It also shows that buffers equivalent to the width of service areas have been removed from planar segments. Furthermore, some large planar segments have been removed due to insufficient solar irradiation. The approach successfully considers factors such as rooftop shape, orientation, superstructures, and occlusions when determining suitable areas for placing photovoltaics.

The study area encompasses a total rooftop area of 4224 m m^2, with 700 m^2 deemed utilizable. Annually, the entire rooftop area generates 403505 kWh of electricity, while the utilizable portions contribute 90105 kWh of electricity. The electricity yield has been estimated using Eq. 1, where the efficiency and performance ratio of the photovoltaics were set to 0.16 and 0.75, respectively. The utilizable areas account for only a small percentage of the total rooftops (16.6%); as a result, evaluating the solar energy potential of buildings based on their entire rooftop areas could result in overestimation.

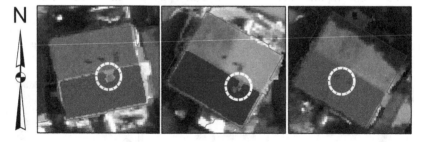

Fig. 5. Utilizable areas of some rooftops. The impact of superstructures is highlighted by white circles.

5   Conclusion and Future Work

Rooftop photovoltaics have acquired a prominent place in cities due to their potential to contribute to energy sustainability. They a have high capacity to reduce carbon emissions and environmental impacts of energy generation. Reliable assessments of rooftop solar potential require finding areas of rooftops where photovoltaics may be installed efficiently. In this study, a procedure was developed to estimate the solar energy potential of rooftops. First, rooftops were extracted from LiDAR point clouds using PointNet++, and their boundaries were regularized. Then, planar segments were extracted based on clustering

and region growing integration. The clustering step requires no prior knowledge regarding the dataset and has an optimized computational speed. In this
step, planarity analysis was also incorporated to enhance clustering. Afterward,
utilizable areas were determined by considering service areas, solar irradiation,
roof shape, and occlusions. The results showed that rooftops and their planar
segments were successfully extracted with 93% accuracy and 88% IOU and 99%
accuracy and 98% IOU, respectively. In addition, it was observed that the shape,
orientation, and superstructures of rooftops and shadow effects were satisfacto-
rily considered in identifying utilizable areas. As a result, the procedure can be
regarded as a reliable way to estimate the solar energy potential of rooftops in
practice.

Although the methods have shown remarkable performance, there is still
room for improvement. The economic feasibility of installing photovoltaics was
not assessed in this study. The economic feasibility assessment involves estimating the costs and benefits of installation, such as the initial installation cost,
maintenance expenses, and potential revenue from surplus power supplied to
the grid. This assessment can aid in identifying the most economically viable
rooftop areas for photovoltaics, considering both the potential for power production and the associated costs and benefits. Another potential direction is to
extend the methods to include the façades of buildings. Our procedure focused
only on rooftops and considered rooftops to be the only areas with the potential
for installing photovoltaics. But façades of buildings can also have the suitable
potential for generating energy. Thus, future work can extend our procedure to
include façades in addition to rooftops.

References

1. Akkiraju, N., Edelsbrunner, H., Facello, M., Fu, P., Mücke, P., E., Varela, C.: Alpha
   shapes: definition and software. In: Proceedings on International Computational
   Geometry Software Workshop, Minneapolis (1995)
2. Aslani, M.: Computational and spatial analyses of rooftops for urban solar energy
   planning. Ph.D. thesis, Gävle University (2022)
3. Aslani, M., Seipel, S.: A fast instance selection method for support vector machines
   in building extraction. Appl. Soft Comput. **97**, 106716 (2020)
4. Aslani, M., Seipel, S.: Efficient and decision boundary aware instance selection for
   support vector machines. Inf. Sci. **577**, 579–598 (2021)
5. Aslani, M., Seipel, S.: A spatially detailed approach to the assessment of rooftop
   solar energy potential based on LiDAR data. In: The 8th International Conference
   on Geographical Information Systems Theory, Applications and Management, pp.
   56–63. SCITEPRESS (2022)
6. Aslani, M., Seipel, S.: Automatic identification of utilizable rooftop areas in digital
   surface models for photovoltaics potential assessment. Appl. Energy **306**(Part A),
   118033 (2022)
7. Benciolini, B., Ruggiero, V., Vitti, A., Zanetti, M.: Roof planes detection via a
   second-order variational model. ISPRS J. Photogram. Remote Sens. **138**, 101–120
   (2018)

8. Bódis, K., Kougias, I., Jäger-Waldau, A., Taylor, N., Szabó, S.: A high-resolution geospatial assessment of the rooftop solar photovoltaic potential in the European Union. Renew. Sustain. Energy Rev. **114**, 109309 (2019)

9. Byrne, J., Taminiau, J., Kurdgelashvili, L., Kim, K.N.: A review of the solar city concept and methods to assess rooftop solar electric potential, with an illustrative application to the city of Seoul. Renew. Sustain. Energy Rev. **41**, 830–844 (2015)

10. Chen, D., Zhang, L., Mathiopoulos, P.T., Huang, X.: A methodology for automated segmentation and reconstruction of urban 3-D buildings from ALS point clouds. IEEE J. Sel. Topics Appl. Earth Obs. Remote Sens. **7**(10), 4199–4217 (2014)

11. Chow, A., Li, S., Fung, A.S.: Modeling urban solar energy with high spatiotemporal resolution: a case study in Toronto, Canada. Int. J. Green Energy **13**(11), 1090–1101 (2016)

12. Deschaud, J.E., Goulette, F.: A fast and accurate plane detection algorithm for large noisy point clouds using filtered normals and voxel growing. In: 3DPVT. Paris, France (2010)

13. Ester, M., Kriegel, H.P., Sander, J., Xu, X.: A density-based algorithm for discovering clusters in large spatial databases with noise. In: the Second International Conference on Knowledge Discovery in Databases and Data Mining, pp. 226–231. AAAI Press, Portland (1996)

14. Fu, P., Rich, P.M.: The Solar Analyst 1.0 Manual. Technical Report, Helios Environmental Modeling Institute (HEMI), USA (2000)

15. Gassar, A.A.A., Cha, S.H.: Review of geographic information systems-based rooftop solar photovoltaic potential estimation approaches at urban scales. Appl. Energy **291**, 116817 (2021)

16. Gilani, S.A.N., Awrangjeb, M., Lu, G.: segmentation of airborne point cloud data for automatic building roof extraction. GISci. Remote Sens. **55**(1), 63–89 (2018)

17. Gribov, A.: Optimal compression of a polyline while aligning to preferred directions. In: 2019 International Conference on Document Analysis and Recognition Workshops (ICDARW), vol. 1, pp. 98–102 (2019). https://doi.org/10.1109/ICDARW.2019.00022

18. Huang, Y., Chen, Z., Wu, B., Chen, L., Mao, W., Zhao, F., Wu, J., Wu, J., Yu, B.: Estimating roof solar energy potential in the downtown area using a GPU-accelerated solar radiation model and airborne LiDAR data. Remote Sens. **7**(12), 17212–17233 (2015)

19. Kingma, D.P., Ba, J.: Adam: a method for stochastic optimization. In: International Conference on Learning Representations (ICLR), Ithaca, San Diego (2015)

20. Lingfors, D., Bright, J.M., Engerer, N.A., Ahlberg, J., Killinger, S., Widén, J.: Comparing the capability of low- and high-resolution LiDAR data with application to solar resource assessment, roof type classification and shading analysis. Appl. Energy **205**, 1216–1230 (2017)

21. Lodha, S., Fitzpatrick, D., Helmbold, D.: Aerial lidar data classification using AdaBoost. In: Proceedings of the International Conference on 3-D Digital Imaging and Modeling, pp. 435–442. IEEE, Montreal, Canada (2007)

22. Lukač, N., Špelič, D., Štumberger, G., Žalik, B.: Optimisation for large-scale photovoltaic arrays' placement based on light detection and ranging data. Appl. Energy **263**, 114592 (2020)

23. Mainzer, K., Killinger, S., McKenna, R., Fichtner, W.: Assessment of rooftop photovoltaic potentials at the urban level using publicly available geodata and image recognition techniques. Solar Energy **155**, 561–573 (2017)

24. Murphy, K.P.: Machine Learning: A Probabilistic Perspective. MIT Press, Cambridge, Massachusetts (2012)

25. Nelson, J.R., Grubesic, T.H.: The use of LiDAR versus unmanned aerial systems (UAS) to assess rooftop solar energy potential. Sustain. Cities Soc. **61**, 102353 (2020)

26. Pavlidis, N.G., Hofmeyr, D.P., Tasoulis, S.K.: Minimum density hyperplanes. J. Mach. Learn. Res. **17**(156), 1–33 (2016)

27. Qi, C.R., Yi, L., Su, H., Guibas, L.J.: PointNet++: deep hierarchical feature learning on point sets in a metric space. In: 31st Conference on Neural Information Processing Systems (NIPS 2017), California (2017)

28. Rich, P., Dubayah, R., Hetrick, W., Saving, S.: Using viewshed models to calculate intercepted solar radiation: applications in ecology. In: American Society for Photogrammetry and Remote Sensing Technical Papers, pp. 524–529 (1994)

29. Romero Rodríguez, L., Duminil, E., Sánchez Ramos, J., Eicker, U.: Assessment of the photovoltaic potential at urban level based on 3D city models: a case study and new methodological approach. Solar Energy **146**, 264–275 (2017)

30. Rusu, R.B.: Semantic 3D Object Maps for Everyday Manipulation in Human Living Environments. Ph.D. thesis, Technical University of Munich, Munich, Germany (2009)

31. Sampath, A., Shan, J.: Segmentation and reconstruction of polyhedral building roofs from aerial LiDAR point clouds. IEEE Trans. Geosci. Remote Sens. **48**(3), 1554–1567 (2010)

32. Schallenberg-Rodríguez, J.: Photovoltaic techno-economical potential on roofs in regions and islands: the case of the canary islands. Methodological review and methodology proposal. Renew. Sustain. Energy Rev. **20**, 219–239 (2013)

33. Shin, Y.H., Son, K.W., Lee, D.C.: semantic segmentation and building extraction from airborne LiDAR data with multiple return using PointNet++. Appl. Sci. **12**(4), 1975 (2022)

34. Sundararajan, D.: Digital Image Processing A Signal Processing and Algorithmic Approach. Springer, Singapore (2017)

35. Thai, C., Brouwer, J.: Challenges estimating distributed solar potential with utilization factors: California universities case study. Appl. Energy **282**, 116209 (2021)

36. Thebault, M., Clivillé, V., Berrah, L., Desthieux, G.: Multicriteria roof sorting for the integration of photovoltaic systems in urban environments. Sustain. Cities Soc. **60**, 102259 (2020)

37. Varney, N., Asari, V.K., Graehling, Q.: DALES: a large-scale aerial LiDAR data set for semantic segmentation. In: 2020 IEEE/CVF Conference on Computer Vision and Pattern Recognition Workshops (CVPRW), pp. 717–726 (2020). https://doi.org/10.1109/CVPRW50498.2020.00101

38. Xie, Y., Tian, J., Zhu, X.X.: Linking points with labels in 3d: a review of point cloud semantic segmentation. IEEE Geosci. Remote Sens. Mag. **8**(4), 38–59 (2020)

39. Xu, Y., Stilla, U.: Toward building and civil infrastructure reconstruction from point clouds: a review on data and key techniques. IEEE J. Sel. Top. Appl. Earth Obser. Remote Sens. **14**, 2857–2885 (2021)

40. Yildirim, D., Büyüksalih, G., ahin, A.D.: Rooftop photovoltaic potential in Istanbul: calculations based on LiDAR data, measurements and verifications. Appl. Energy **304**, 117743 (2021)

41. Zheng, Y., Weng, Q.: Model-driven reconstruction of 3-d buildings using LiDAR data. IEEE Geosci. Remote Sens. Lett. **12**(7), 1541–1545 (2015)

Author Index

C. Grueau et al. (Eds.): GISTAM 2021/2022, CCIS 1908, p. 117, 2023.
https://doi.org/10.1007/978-3-031-44112-7

Printed in the United States
by Baker & Taylor Publisher Services